Harriet Waters Preston, Frédéric Mistral

Mirèio

A Provençal Poem

Harriet Waters Preston, Frédéric Mistral

Mirèio
A Provençal Poem

ISBN/EAN: 9783744718868

Printed in Europe, USA, Canada, Australia, Japan

Cover: Foto ©Thomas Meinert / pixelio.de

More available books at **www.hansebooks.com**

Mirèio.

A PROVENÇAL POEM.

by

FRÉDÉRIC MISTRAL.

Translated by

Harriet Waters Preston.

CAMEO SERIES

T. FISHER UNWIN   PATERNOSTER SQ.
LONDON E.C. MDCCCXC

To Lamartine.

Te consecre Mirèio : es moun cor e moun amo,
*   Es la flour de mis an.*
Es un raisin de crau qu'emé touto sa ramo,
*   Te porge un païsan.*

———

I offer thee Mirèio : it is my heart and spirit,
*   The blossom of my years.*
A cluster of Crau grapes, with all the green leaves
*   near it,*
*   To thee a peasant bears.*

THIRTY odd years have come and gone since the curious *litterateurs* of Paris were excited and charmed by the apparition of Frédéric Mistral's " Mirèio." A pastoral poem in twelve cantos, composed in the dialect of the *Bouches du Rhône,* and first issued by an obscure bookseller at Avignon, it was produced before the great literary world with a parallel French version of the author's own, very singular and rather *sauvage* as French, but exceedingly bold, picturesque, and poetic, and the poem had the further advantage of a most eloquent and sympathetic introduction in the *Revue des Deux Mondes,* of September 15, 1859, by Saint-René Taillandier.

The employment of a rustic southern dialect for the purposes of poetic narrative was by no means so unheard-of a thing, even to the men of that generation, as was indirectly assumed by the first reviewer of " Mirèio." Had not Jacques Jasmin, the immortal barber of Agen, written, in his own local *patois*, " Françonette," and " The Blind Girl of Castel Cuillé," and the inimitable " Papillotes " ? But the work of Mistral, along with that of the school which he claimed to represent, and of which he was easily chief, was heralded by a certain *fanfare*—it came with a specific and impressive claim of ancient Provençal traditions to be revived, and a vast future inaugurated : pretensions which would have seemed almost droll to the Gascon Jasmin, with his exquisite humour and his adorable simplicity.

I can do no more than glance in this place at the history of the self-styled Provençal Revival, the most ambibitious and by far the most romantic literary adventure of our day. It is an inviting subject, and will one day form an interesting chapter in the long annals of poesy ; but the time is not yet fully come for estimating its results, and still less, with its greatest champion yet living, for writing its obituary.

Joseph Roumanille, a schoolmaster of St. Remy, near Tarascon, was the father of the movement. He first wrote poems in modern Provençal, so the pleasant legend says, because his old mother could not understand him when he essayed to read her those which he had written in French. Delighted, and, as it would seem, a little amazed at his own success, he came forward as the rightful heir to the long-lapsed inheritance of the Troubadours, assumed that the language, whose literary capacities he had re-discovered, was essentially the same as theirs, and contrived thoroughly to imbue with his own faith in its future a band of clever and ardent pupils, among whom, by the will of Heaven, there was one rare genius—Frédéric Mistral, and one wild enthusiast, who was, at the same time, an affluent and pathetic versifier—Théodore Aubanel. Animated by a mystical assurance, hardly less profound than that of Loyola and his companions upon Montmartre, these knights of song bound themselves by a sort of vow, to write in the effete language of the French Academy no more. They constituted themselves a poetic order, and proceeded to adopt an elaborate and somewhat fantastic organization. The almost religious earnestness which animated them may be judged by the fact that when one of the original band, Eugène Garcin—formally saluted by name, along with some half-dozen others, in the sixth canto of "Mirèio—cooled in his ardour a little, and attempted to point out the factitious and impracticable side of the movement, he was solemnly denounced by Mistral as "the Judas of our litttle church." It was a defection of no serious moment, and the revival went its fervid way without Garcin.

The Provençal poets agreed to call themselves *felibre*, nobody knows to this day exactly why. There are those who say that the word means *homme de foi libre*, that is, emancipated from all slavish literary tradition—as Mistral and his first associates undoubtedly were ; there are sticklers for antiquity and a direct descent from the Latin, who maintain the derivation *qui facit libros*. Howbeit the *felibre* began to publish at Avignon in the speech of the district, a periodical, which still, I think, appears at irregular intervals. They constructed a small grammar on the lines of the existing grammars of the ancient " Langue d'oc," especially of Raynouard's " Résumé de la Grammaire Romaine," and they began the compilation of an extensive dictionary, which has never even approached completion. They also revived the institution of an annual poetic tournament with floral prizes—a silver lily, a golden violet—where the

A*

native bards recited their verses, and received their rewards, after the supposed manner of the olden time. These jousts were usually held in the late summer or the early autumn. There were others appointed for the yet more appropriate month of May, which received the name of the feast of the *Santo Estello*, or Holy Star,—*memourativo de la reneissenço dou Gai-Sabe*—to commemorate the renascence of the Gay Science. Once in seven years this feast was to be celebrated with extraordinary splendour, "in honour" (I continue to quote from the address of Mistral at the Floral Games held at Hyères in 1885) " of the seven rays of that mysterious star which leads, whithersoever God will, our bark with its orange-freight." That is to say, which determines, after the manner of the Star of Bethlehem, the place where our society shall assemble and listen to the pieces entered for competition.

Were it possible for a new language to be created, or a decaying one revived, of determinate purpose, by native genius, fiery enthusiasm and unstinted devotion to the cause, that miracle would surely have been wrought by the *felibre* of the *Bouches du Rhône*. But the triumph of a language, like that of the kingdom of heaven, is among the things which do not come by observation. It is determined by causes as vast as those which shape the continents, and quite as independent of the theories of individual men. The order of the Holy Star, was after all only a kind of idealized mutual admiration society, and of all its members during a full quarter of a century, three names only have advanced from local renown to anything like general recognition.

They are the three names already cited of Roumanille, Aubanel, and Mistral.

The two former have already passed away, leaving behind them many charming lyrics, but no work of universal and lasting interest. Mistral is gloriously young at sixty, able, and let us hope willing, to give us in that rich and flowing idiom, which no one else has ever managed with such mastery as he, many more historical and narrative poems, vivid with local colour, and teeming with local tradition, like " Calendau "—a romance of the last century, which appeared in 1873 and " Nerto " —a tale of the time of the Popes at Avignon, published in 1884. But it is safe to prophesy that neither Mistral nor any other *felibre* will ever give us another " Mirèio "—so spontaneous, artless, and impassioned, so dewy with the memories of the poet's own childhood on a Provençal farm, or *mas*, so gay with the laughter and moving with the tears of simple folk, reflecting in so flawless a mirror every change of the seasons, every aspect of the free, primitive, bucolic life of the Mediterranean shore.

The success of Aubanel was perhaps frustrated by the very extravagance of his own aims. When we find him at the *fêtes* of Forcalquier in 1875 apostrophizing the arbiters of literary renown in France in terms like these : " Sachez que nous sommes un grand peuple, et qu'il n'est plus temps de nous mépriser. Trente départements parlent notre langue, d'une mer à l'autre mer, des Pyrénées jusqu'aux Alpes, de Crau à Limousin ; le même amour fait battre notre poitrine, l'amour de la terre natale et de la langue maternelle . . . Sachez que vous serez tombés longtemps alors

que le Provençal, toujours jeune, parlera encore
de vous avec pitié "—we can then understand that
Saint-René Tallandier, the original sponsor of
Mirèio, should have made haste to express his
grave apprehensions for the sanity of the revival-
ist movement, and to repudiate in the name of
of the great Review all countenance of so vast a
pretension on behalf of an "idiom ˙ which had
vanished for six hundred years from the battle-
field of ideas."

One is reminded of the lament of the late
William Barnes that the dialect of Dorset had
not prevailed in England over the tongue of
Shakespeare. Yet William Barnes, like the *felibre*,
wrote poems in the local *patois*, far more beautiful and pathetic than any which he ever produced
in proper English.

Mistral himself, with the profounder instincts
and wiser judgment of a really large mind, has
grown more modest from year to year in his hopes
concerning the final harvest of that generous enter-
prise to which his life and powers have been con-
secrated. He was not quite able to extend a hearty
welcome to Alphonse Daudet, when that most
humane and sympathetic of realists appeared upon
the scene with "Numa Roumestan" and the
"Lettres de mon Moulin," describing in the most
pellucid French and with a fidelity equal to his
own, the prose aspect of the life of the South, and
all the rustic scenes which Mistral had so affec-
tionately poetized. All the *felibre*, indeed, looked
askance at Daudet as an intruder, and this is one
more sign, if not of the limitations of their leader's
genius, at least of the narrow and ephemeral
character of their collective ideal. However, in an

address delivered before the previously-mentioned
assembly at Hyères in 1885 — ten years after
Aubanel had hurled his fierce defiance at the
French Academy—Mistral might have been heard
pleading, with much earnestness and good sense,
that French and Provençal should be kept reso-
lutely distinct, both in the teaching of the schools,
and in the talk of the people, and that, by way of
preserving the purity of *both forms of speech.*

His remarks had an especial appropriateness
then and there, because the prose work crowned
upon that occasion was a series of naïve and highly
dramatic dialogues, entitled "Scènes de la Vie
Provençale," by M. C. Sénès, of Toulon, officially
known as La Sinse.   French of the most barbaric,
and Provençal of the most pliant, are mixed up in
these delightfully comic dialogues exactly as they
are upon the lips of the common folk.   It is the
most amusing, perhaps the only distinctly amusing
work which the school of the *felibre* has ever produced, and anybody who reads French may read
and have a hearty laugh over it.   And I may add,
from my own experience, that a very short residence
in the ancient Provincia is enough to show that the
local idiom is much more intelligible phonetically
than it looks at first sight upon paper.

I may be mistaken, but I take the truth to be
that modern Provençal is, after all, a dialect only,
and not, as was so long and passionately claimed
by the confederate poets, a language.   As a matter
of fact, it resembles the plastic idiom of the ancient
Troubadours very little more than it resembles
modern French, and certainly no more than it
resembles Gascon, Catalan, or the Italian of the
Western Riviera.   All the Romance dialects, how-

ever fallen from literary honour, or untamed by literary law, are closely akin, and bear marks, even in their utmost degradation, of the same illustrious pedigree. They are like certain wild flowers, the pimpernel, the anemone, whose species can never be mistaken, but whose colours present, and that spontaneously, an almost infinite variety.

The poem of " Mirèio," in parallel French and Provençal, first fell in my way in the summer of 1871 ; and I admire my own audacity in immediately attempting to turn it into English verse,[1] almost as much as I do that of the men who first preached the Provençal crusade against the language of Racine and Molière. Of course I knew no more of the idiom in which it was originally composed than could be gathered from a close comparison of the same with Mistral's own French, aided by a smattering of old Provençal. I may plead in extenuation of my effrontery that there was virtually no more to be known at that time, for even the grammar already mentioned had not then been published. There is not very much more to be known even now.

The scheme of the Provençal verse, though elaborate, and seemingly very artificial, was easily enough intelligible to an English ear ; more so, I should fancy, than to a Parisian one, on account of its obvious *jingle*—or, to speak by the book, the exuberance of its rhymes, and the strength of its tonic accents. The same remark, as is well known, applies in a general way to the songs of the Troubadours. Mistral's stanza consists of five eight-syllabled iambic lines with feminine rhymes, in groups of two and three, and two twelve-syllabled

[1] Boston, U.S.A., Roberts Bros., 1872.

iambic lines, with masculine rhymes.   The Quaker
poet Whittier had fallen upon a somewhat similar
verse, in one of the finest of his earlier poems—
" Lines written at Hampton Beach " :—

> " So when Time's veil shall fall asunder,
>   The soul may know
> No sudden change, no curious wonder,
> Nor sink the weight of mystery under,
>   But with the upward rise, and with the vastness grow."

But this is far simpler than Mistral's.

I did actually make an attempt to transfer this
florid measure to our own sober English tongue,
and that eminent American poet and very dis-
tinguished connoisseur in poetic metres, the late
Mr. Longfellow, once told me that he greatly wished
I had persevered, and that he thought it would
have been quite possible to render the whole poem
in the same way.   Perhaps it would have been,
to a master of versification, like himself ; and
for his sake, and out of respect for his opinion, I
subjoin the opening stanzas of the poem in Provençal, and my own attempt to imitate their metre,
premising, for the benefit of the unskilled, that in
Provençal every letter sounds, the vowels as in
French, while of the consonants *g* and *j* before *e*
and *i* are pronounced like *ds*, and *ch* always like *ts*.
A final vowel is elided, in scanning, before another
vowel ; and the tonic accent is strongly marked :—

> " Cante uno chato de Prouvènço,
>   Dins lis amour de la jouvènço,
> A travès da la Crau, vers la mar, dins li bla,
>   Umble escoulan d'ou grand Oumero,
>   Iéu la vole segui.   Coume èro
>   Rèn qu'uno chato de Prouvènço,
> En foro de la Crau se n'es gaire parla.

> Emai soun front noun lusiguèsse
> Que de jouinesso ; emai n'agùesse
> Ni diadèmo d'or ni mantèu de Damas,
> Vole qu'en glòri fugue aussado
> Coune uno rèino, e caressado
> Pèr nosto lengo mespresado
> Car cantan que pèr vautre, o pastre e gènt dì mas ! "

Or thus :—

> " A maiden of Provence I sing ;
> I tell the love-tale of her spring,
> Across La Crau's wide wheat-fields follow her to the sea.
> Mine be the daring aspiration
> To sing of her in Homer's fashion,
> My lady of the lowly station,
> Unknown beyond the prairies of lone La Crau was she.
>
> What though her brow was never crowned
> Save with the youth that rayed it round ?
> What though she bore no golden crown and wore no damask
>   cloak ?
> Yet I would have her raised in glory
> As a queen is, and set before me
> In our poor speech to tell her story,
> Because I sing for you alone, shepherds and farmer-folk ! "

To me the thought of keeping this up for twelve cantos was simply appalling. Even in my trial stanzas, as will be seen, I had sacrificed many of the feminine rhymes ; and I am now inclined to think, though I speak under correction, that Mistral himself and his followers availed themselves pretty liberally of the license which the classic Troubadours are well known to have employed, of manipulating their final syllables more or less in order to make them rhyme.

The measure finally adopted — ten-syllabled iambic lines with consecutive rhymes, usually masculine but sometimes feminine—was essentially the same as that employed by William Morris in the " Earthly Paradise." That beautiful work was then new, and very popular in America, and it seemed, and I own that to me it seems still, to present almost the ideal of English narrative poetry. But I broke my version into stanzas of six lines, by way, I suppose, of making it look more like the original.

In those comparatively early days, I also held, and rather doated on, a theory of my own about what are called imperfect rhymes. I was persuaded that rhymes where the consonant sounds correspond while the vowel sounds merely approximate—like *wreck* and *make*, *gone* and *son*—are the counterpart on the one hand of assonances upon the other, in which the vowels correspond but not the consonants ; that their relation to perfect rhymes is exactly that of minor to major harmonies, and that they relieve the ear in a long-rhymed poem, no less than the latter in a musical composition. Though very naturally censured for the freedom with which I exercised this caprice in my version of "Mirèio," I still clung to it tenaciously as late as 1880, when I made a version of the Georgics of Vergil. I am by no means certain even now that there is not sound musical justification for the idea, but I have grown conservative with years, as we are all apt to do, and I cherish an ever-increasing respect for *law*—literary and other. In the present edition of my " Mirèio," I have therefore reformed and, so to speak, *ranged* some scores of these licentious rhymes, aiming always, at the same time, at coming closer to the meaning of the original, as I now understand it, even if need be, at the sacrifice of some picturesqueness in the English line.

I had always beside me when I first made my version, the English prose translation of "Mirèio," by Mr. C. H. Grant, to which I feel myself to have been not a little indebted. In artlessness of narrative, in vigour and felicity of expression, I have never hoped to surpass this unrhymed and un-measured version, which needed, as it seemed to me, only a rhythmic form to render it worthy of the essentially *musical* original.

A second English translation, by H. Crichton, with which I became acquainted subsequently, had been published by Macmillan and Co., London, in 1868. This version was a metrical one, and fairly close, but it failed, I think, in catching, not the music merely, but the rural freshness and fragrance, the genuinely bucolic spirit of the Provençal. It is because, I venture to hope, that my version, with all its faults, does reflect something of all this, that a new edition of it is offered to the public after so long a time.

HARRIET WATERS PRESTON.

BRUSSELS,
    April, 1890.

Contents.

Contents

CANTO I.

Lotus Farm.

I SING the love of a Provençal maid ;
  How through the wheat-fields of La Crau she
    strayed,
Following the fate that drew her to the sea.
Unknown beyond remote La Crau was she ;
And I, who tell the rustic tale of her,
Would fain be Homer's humble follower.

What though youth's aureóle was her only crown ?
And never gold she wore nor damask gown ?
I'll build her up a throne out of my song,
And hail her queen in our despisèd tongue.
Mine be the simple speech that ye all know,
Shepherds and farmer-folk of lone La Crau.

God of my country, who didst have Thy birth
Among poor shepherds when Thou wast on earth,
Breathe fire into my song ! Thou knowest, my God,
How, when the lusty summer is abroad,
And figs turn ripe in sun and dew, comes he,—
Brute, greedy man,—and quite despoils the tree.

Yet on that ravaged tree thou savest oft
Some little branch inviolate aloft,
Tender and airy up against the blue,
Which the rude spoiler cannot win unto :
Only the birds shall come and banquet there,
When, at St. Magdalene's, the fruit is fair.

Methinks I see yon airy little bough :
It mocks me with its freshness even now ;
The light breeze lifts it, and it waves on high
Fruitage and foliage that cannot die.
Help me, dear God, on our Provençal speech,
To soar until the birds' own home I reach !

Once, then, beside the poplar-bordered Rhone,
There lived a basket-weaver and his son,
In a poor hut set round with willow-trees
(For all their humble wares were made from these) ;
And sometimes they from farm to farm would wend,
And horses' cribs and broken baskets mend.

And so one evening, as they trudged their round
With osier bundles on their shoulders bound,
" Father," young Vincen said, " the clouds look wild
About old Magalouno's tower up-piled.
If that gray rampart fell, 'twould do us harm :
We should be drenched ere we had gained the farm."

" Nay, nay ! " the old man said, " no rain to-night !
'Tis the sea-breeze that shakes the trees.   All right !
A western gale were different."   Vincen mused :
" Are many ploughs at Lotus farmstead used ? "
" Six ploughs ! " the basket-weaver answered slow :
" It is the finest freehold in La Crau.

" Look !   There's their olive-orchard, intermixt
With rows of vines and almond-trees betwixt.
The beauty of it is, that vineyard hath
For every day in all the year a path !
There's ne'er another such the beauty is ;
And in each path are just so many trees."

" O heavens !   How many hands at harvest-tide
So many trees must need ! " young Vincen cried.

" Nay : for 'tis almost Hallowmas, you know,
When all the girls come flocking in from Baux,
And, singing, heap with olives green and dun
The sheets and sacks, and call it only fun."

The sun was sinking, as old Ambroi said ;
On high were little clouds a-flush with red ;
Sideways upon their yokèd cattle rode
The labourers slowly home, each with his goad
Erect.   Night darkened on the distant moor ;
'Twas supper-time, the day of toil was o'er.

" And here we are ! " the boy cried.   " I can see
The straw-heaped threshing-floor, so hasten we ! "
" But stay ! " the other.   " Now, as I'm alive,
The Lotus Farm's the place for sheep to thrive,—
The pine-woods all the summer, and the sweep
Of the great plain in winter.   Lucky sheep !

" And look at the great trees that shade the dwelling,
And look at that delicious stream forth welling
Inside the vivary !   And mark the bees !
Autumn makes havoc in their colonies ;
But every year, when comes the bright May weather,
Yon lotus-grove a hundred swarms will gather."

" And one thing more ! " cried Vincen, eagerly,
" The very best of all, it seems to me,—
I mean the maiden, father, who dwells here.
Thou canst not have forgotten how, last year,
She bade us bring her olive-baskets two,
And fit her little one with handles new."

So saying, they drew the farm-house door a-nigh,
And, in the dewy twilight, saw thereby
The maid herself.   Distaff in hand she stood,
Watching her silk-worms at their leafy food.
Then master Ambroi let his osiers fall,
And sang out cheerily, " Good-even, all ! "

" Father, the same to you ! " the damsel said.
" I had come out my distaff-point to thread,
It grows so dark.   Whence come you now, I pray ?
From Valabrègo ? "   Ambroi answered, " Yea.
I said, when the fast-coming dark I saw,
' We'll sleep at Lotus Farm upon the straw.' "

Whereat, with no more words, father and son
Hard by upon a roller sat them down,
And fell to their own work right busily.
A half-made cradle chanced the same to be.
Fast through the nimble fingers of the two
The supple osier bent and crossed and flew.

Certes, our Vincen was a comely lad.
A bright face and a manly form he had,
Albeit that summer he was bare sixteen.
Swart were his cheeks ; but the dark soil, I ween,
Bears the fine wheat, and black grapes make the wine
That sets our feet a-dance, our eyes a-shine.

Full well he knew the osier to prepare,
And deftly wrought : but ofttimes to his share
Fell coarser work ; for he the panniers made
Wherewith the farmers use their beasts to lade,
And divers kinds of baskets, huge and rough,
Handy and light.   Ay, he had skill enough !

And likewise brooms of millet-grass, and such,—
And baskets of split-cane.   And still his touch
Was sure and swift ; and all his wares were strong,
And found a ready sale the farms among.
But now, from fallow field and moorland vast,
The labourers were trooping home at last.

Then hasted sweet Mirèio to prepare,
With her own hands and in the open air,

Their evening meal. There was a broad flat stone
Served for a table, and she set thereon
One mighty dish, where each man plunged his ladle.
Our weavers wrought meanwhile upon their cradle.

Until Ramoun, the master of the farm,
Cried, " How is this ? "—brusque was his tone and warm.
" Come to your supper, Ambroi : no declining !
Put up the crib, my man : the stars are shining.
And thou, Mirèio, run and fetch a bowl :
The travellers must be weary, on my soul ! "

Wherefore the basket-weaver, well-content,
Rose with his son and to the table went,
And sat him down and cut the bread for both ;
While bright Mirèio hasted, nothing loth,
Seasoned a dish of beans with olive oil,
And came and sat before them with a smile.

Not quite fifteen was this same fair Mirèio.
Ah, me ! the purple coast of Font Vièio,
The hills of Baux, the desolate Crau plain,
A shape like hers will hardly see again.
Child of the merry sun, her dimpled face
Bloomed into laughter with ingenious grace.

Eyes had she limpid as the drops of dew ;
And, when she fixed their tender gaze on you,
Sorrow was not. Stars in a summer night
Are not more softly, innocently bright :
And beauteous hair, all waves and rings of jet ;
And breasts, a double peach, scarce ripened yet.

Shy, yet a joyous little sprite she was ;
And, finding all her sweetness in a glass,
You would have drained it at a single breath.
·But to our tale, which somewhat lingereth.
When every man his day's toil had rehearsed
(So, at my father's farm, I heard them first),—

B

"Now, Ambroi, for a song!" they all began:
"Let us not sleep above our supper, man!"
But he, "Peace! peace! My friends, do ye not know
On every jester, God, they say, doth blow
And sets him spinning like a top along?
Sing yourselves, lads,—you who are young and strong."

"No jest, good father, none!" they answered him.
"But, since the wine o'erflows your goblet's brim,
Drink with us, Ambroi, and then to your song!"
"Ay, ay, when I was young—but that was long
Ago—I'd sing to any man's desire;
But now my voice is but a broken lyre."

"But, Master Ambroi," urged Mirèio,
"Sing one song, please, because 'twill cheer us so."
"My pretty one," the weaver said again,
"Only the husks of my old voice remain;
But if these please you, I cannot say nay,"
And drained his goblet, and began straightway :—

I.

Our Captain was Bailly Suffren;
　　We had sailed from Toulon,
Five hundred sea-faring Provençaux,
　　Stout-hearted and strong :

'Twas the sweet hope of meeting the English that made
　　our hearts burn,
And till we had thrashed them we vowed we would never
　　return.

II.

But all the first month of our cruise
　　We saw never a thing
From the shrouds, save hundreds and hundreds
　　Of gulls on the wing;
And in the next dolorous month, we'd a tempest to fight,
And had to be bailing out water by day and by night.

III.

By the third, we were driven to madness
  At meeting no foe
For our thundering cannon to sweep
  From the ocean. When lo !
"Hands aloft !" Captain cried. At the maintop one
  heard the command,
And the long Arab coast on the lee-bow intently he
  scanned.

IV.

Till, "God's thunder !" he cried. "Three big ve:sels
  Bear down on us strong ;
Run the guns to the ports ! Blaze away ! "
  Shouted Bailly Suffren.
"Sharp's the word, gallant lads ! Our figs of Antibes
  they shall test,
And see how they like those," Captain said, " ere we
  offer the rest ! "

V.

A crash fit to deafen ! Before
  The words left his lips
We had sent forty balls through the hulls
  Of the Englishers' ships !
One was done for already. And now the guns only
  heard we,
The cracking of wood and perpetual groan of the sea.

VI.

And now we were closing. Oh, rapture !
  We lay alongside,
Our gallant commander stood cool
  On the deck, and he cried,
" Well done, my brave boys ! But enough ! Cease your
  firing, I say,
For the time has come now to anoint them with oil of
  Aix."

VII.

Then we sprang to our dirks and our hatchets,
    As they had been toys ;
And, grapnel in hand, the Provençal
    Cried, "Board 'em, my boys ! "
A shout and a leap, and we stood on the Englishers'
    deck ;
And then, ah, 'twas then we were ready our vengeance
    to wreak !

VIII.

Then, oh, the great slaughter ! The crash
    Of the mainmast ensuing !
And the blows and the turmoil of men
    Fighting on 'mid the ruin !
More than one wild Provençal I saw seize a foe in his
    place,
And hug till he strained his own life out in deadly
    embrace.

And then old Ambroi paused. " Ah, yes ! " said he,
" You do not quite believe my tale, I see.
Nathless these things all happened, understand :
Did I not hold the tiller with this hand ?
Were I to live a thousand years, I say,
I should remember what befell that day."

" What, father, you were there and saw the fun ? "
The labourers cried in mischief. " Three to one,
They flattened you like scythes beneath the hammer ! "
" Who, me ? The English ? " the old tar 'gan stammer,
Upspringing ; then, with smile of fine disdain,
Took up the burden of his tale again :—

IX.

So with blood-dabbled feet fought we on
    Four hours, until dark.
Then, our eyes being cleared of the powder,
    We missed from our bark

Fivescore men. But the king of the English lost ships
of renown :
Three good vessels with all hands on board to the bottom
went down.

X.

And now, our sides riddled with shot,
  Once more homeward hie we,
Yards splintered, mast shivered, sails tattered ;
  But brave Captain Bailly
Spake us words of good cheer. " My comrades, ye have
done well !
To the great king of Paris the tale of your valour I'll tell ! "

XI.

" Well said, Captain dear ! " we replied :
  " Sure the king will hear you
When you speak. But for us, his poor mariners,
  What will he do,—
Who left our all gladly, our homes and our firesides," we
said,
" For his sake, and lo ! now in those homes there is
crying for bread ?

XII.

" Ah, Admiral, never forget
  When all bow before you,
With a love like the love of your seamen
  None will adore you !
Why, say but the word, and, ere homeward our footsteps
we turn,
Aloft on the tips of our fingers a king you are borne ! "

XIII.

A Martigau, mending his nets
  One eve, made this ditty.
Our admiral bade us farewell,
  And sought the great city.

Were they wroth with his glory up there at the court?
     Who can say?
But we saw our beloved commander no more from that
     day!

A timely ending thus the minstrel made,
Else the fast-coming tears his tale had stayed;
But for the labourers—they sat intent,
Mute all, with parted lips, and forward bent
As if enchanted.   Even when he was done,
For a brief space they seemed to hearken on.

"And such were aye the songs," said the old man,
" Sung in the good old days when Martha span.
Long-winded, maybe, and the tunes were queer.
But, youngsters, what of that?   They suit my ear.
Your new French airs mayhap may finer be;
But no one understands the words, you see!"

Whereon the men, somewhat as in a dream,
From table rose, and to the running stream
They led their patient mules, six yoke in all.
The long vine-branches from a trellised wall
Waved o'er them waiting, and, from time to time,
Humming some fragment of the weaver's rhyme.

Mirèio tarried, but not quite alone.
A social spirit had the little one,
And she and Vincen chatted happily.
Twas a fair sight, the two young heads to see
Meeting and parting, coming still and going
Like aster-flowers when merry winds are blowing.

"Now tell me, Vincen," thus Mirèio,
" If oftentimes as you and Ambrio go
Bearing your burdens the wild country over,
Some haunted castle you do not discover,
Or joyous fête, or shining palace meet,
While the home-nest is evermore our seat."

" 'Tis even so, my lady, as you think.
Why, currants quench the thirst as well as drink !
What though we brave all weathers in our toil ?
Sure, we have joys that rain-drops cannot spoil
The sun of noon beats fiercely on the head,
But there are wayside trees unnumberèd.

" And whenso'er return the summer hours,
And olive-trees are all bedecked with flowers,
We hunt the whitening orchards curiously,
Still following the scent, till we descry
In the hot noontide, by its emerald flash,
The tiny cantharis upon the ash.

" The shops will buy the same.   Or off we tramp
And gather red-oak apples in the swamp,
Or beat the pond for leeches.   Ah, that's grand !
You need nor bait nor hook, but only stand
And strike the water, and then one by one
They come and seize your legs, and all is done.

" And thou wert never at Li Santo even !
Dear heart !   The singing there must be like heaven.
'Tis there they bring the sick from all about
For healing ; and the church is small, no doubt :
But, ah, what cries they lift ! what vows they pay
To the great saints !   We saw it one fête-day.

" It was the year of the great miracle.
My God, that was a sight !   I mind it well.
A feeble boy, beautiful as Saint John,
Lay on the pavement, sadly calling on
The saints to give sight to his poor blind eyes,
And promising his pet lamb in sacrifice.

" ' My little lamb, with budding horns !' he said,
' Dear saints !'   How we all wept !   Then from o'erhead

The blessed reliquaries came down slowly,
Above the throngèd people bending lowly,
And crying, 'Come, great saints, mighty and good!
Come, save!' The church was like a wind-swept wood.

"Then the godmother held the child aloft,
Who spread abroad his fingers pale and soft,
And passionately grasped the reliquaries
That held the bones of the three blessed Maries;
Just as a drowning man, who cannot swim,
Will clutch a plank the sea upheaves to him.

"And then, oh! then,—I saw it with these eyes,—
By faith illumined, the blind boy outcries,
' I see the sacred relics, and I see
Grandmother all in tears! Now haste,' said he,
' My lambkin with the budding horns to bring
To the dear saints for a thank-offering!'

"But thou, my lady, God keep thee, I pray,
Handsome and happy as thou art to-day!
Yet if a lizard, wolf, or horrid snake
Ever should wound thee with its fang, betake
Thyself forthwith tô the most holy saints,
Who cure all ills and hearken all complaints."

So the hours of the summer evening passed.
Hard-by the big-wheeled cart its shadow cast
On the white yard. Afar arose and fell
The frequent tinkle of a little bell
In the dark marsh: a nightingale sang yonder;
An owl made dreamy, sorrowful rejoinder.

"Now, since the night is moonlit, so the mere
And trees are glorified, wilt thou not hear,"
The boy besought, "the story of a race
In which I hoped to win the prize?"—"Ah, yes!"
The little maiden sighed; and, more than glad,
Still gazed with parted lips upon the lad.

"Well, then, Mirèio, once at Nismes," he said,
"They had foot-races on the esplanade ;
And on a certain day a crowd was there
Collected, thicker than a shock of hair.
Some shoeless, coatless, hatless, were to run :
The others only came to see the fun.

"When all at once upon the scene appears
One Lagalanto, prince of foot-racers.
In all Provence, and even in Italy,
The fleetest-footed far behind left he.
Yes : Lagalanto, the great Marseillais,—
Thou wilt have heard his name before to-day.

"A leg, a thigh, he had would not look small
By John of Cossa's, the great seneschal ;
And in his dresser many a pewter plate,
With all his victories carved thereon in state ;
And you'd have said, to see his scarfs, my lady,
A wainscot all festooned with rainbows had he.

"The other runners, of whate'er condition,
Threw on their clothes at this dread apparition :
The game was up when Lagalanto came.
Only one stout-limbed lad, Lou Cri by name,
Who into Nismes had driven cows that day,
Durst challenge the victorious Marseillais.

"Whereon, 'Oh, bah !' cried foolish little I
(Just think !—I only chanced to stand thereby),
'I can run too !'   Forthwith they all surround me :
'Run, then !'   Alas ! my foolish words confound me ;
For I had run with partridges alone,
And only the old oaks for lookers-on.

"But now was no escape.   'My poor boy, hasten,'
Says Lagalanto, 'and your latchets fasten.'

B*

Well, so I did.   And the great man meanwhile
Drew o'er his mighty muscles, with a smile,
A pair of silken hose, whereto were sewn
Ten tiny golden bells of sweetest tone.

" So 'twas we three.   Each set between his teeth
A bit of willow, thus to save his breath ;
Shook hands all round ; then, one foot on the line,
Trembling and eager we await the sign
For starting.   It is given.   Off we fly ;
We scour the plain like mad,—'tis you ! 'tis I !

" Wrapped in a cloud of dust, with smoking hair,
We strain each nerve.   Ah, what a race was there !
They thought we should have won the goal abreast,
Till I, presumptuous, sprang before the rest :
And that was my undoing ; for I dropped
Pale, dying as it seemed.   But never stopped

" The others.   On, on, on, with steady gait,
Just like the pasteboard horses at Aix fête.
The famous Marseillais thought he must win
(They used to say of him he had no spleen) ;
But, ah ! my lady, on that day of days,
He found his man,—Lou Cri of Mouriès.

" For now they pass beyond the gazing line,
And almost touch the goal.   O beauty mine !
Couldst thou have seen Lou Cri leap forward then !
Never, I think, in mountain, park, or glen,
A stag, a hare, so fleet of foot you'd find.
Howled like a wolf the other, just behind.

" Lou Cri is victor !—hugs the post for joy.
Then all of Nismes comes flocking round the boy,
To learn the birthplace of this wondrous one.
The pewter plate is flashing in the sun,
The hautboys flourish, cymbals clang apace,
As he receives the guerdon of the race."

"And Lagalanto?" asks Mirèio.
"Why, he upon the ground was sitting low,
Powdered with dust, the shifting folk among,
Clasping his knees.　With shame his soul was wrung
And, with the drops that from his forehead fell,
Came tears of bitterness unspeakable.

"Lou Cri approached, and made a modest bow.
'Brother, let's to the ale-house arbour now,
Behind the amphitheatre.　Why borrow,
Upon this festive day, tears for the morrow?
The money left we'll drink together thus:
There's sunshine yet enough for both of us.'

"Then trembling rose the runner of Marseilles,
And from his limbs made haste to tear away
The silken hose, the golden bells.　'Here, lad
Raising his pallid face, 'take them!' he said.
'I am grown old; youth decks thee like a swan;
So put the strong man's gear with honour on.

"He turned, stricken like an ash the storm bereaves
In summer-time of all its tower of leaves.
The king of runners vanished from the place;
And never more ran he in any race,
Nor even leaped on the inflated hide,
In games at Saint John's or St. Peter's tide."

So Vincen told the story, waxing warm,
Of all he'd seen, before the Lotus Farm.
His cheeks grew red, his eyes were full of light;
He waved his hand to point his speech aright,—
Abundant was the same as showers in May
That fall upon a field of new-mown hay.

The crickets, chirruping amid the dew,
Paused more than once to listen.　Often, too,

The bird of evening, the sweet nightingale,
Kept silence ; thrilling so at Vincen's tale,
As aye she harked her leafy perch upon,
She might have kept awake until the dawn.

"Oh, mother ! " cried Mirèio, "surely never
Was weaver-lad so marvellously clever !
I love to sleep, dear, on a winter night ;
But now I cannot,—it is all too light.
Ah, just one story more before we go,
For I could pass a lifetime listening so ! "

CANTO II.

The Leaf-picking.

SING, magnarello, merrily,
    As the green leaves you gather !
In their third sleep the silk-worms lie,
    And lovely is the weather
Like brown bees that in open glades
    From rosemary gather honey,
The mulberry-trees swarm full of maids,.
    Glad as the air is sunny !

It chanced one morn—it was May's loveliest—
Mirèio gathered leaves among the rest.
It chanced, moreover, on that same May morning,.
The little gypsy, for her own adorning,
Had cherries in her ears, for rings, suspended,
Just as our Vincen's footsteps thither tended.

Like Latin seaside people everywhere,
He wore a red cap on his raven hair,
With a cock's feather gayly set therein ;
And, prancing onward, with a stick made spin
The flints from wayside stone-heaps, and set flying
The lazy adders in his pathway lying.

When suddenly, from the straight, leafy alley,
" Whither so fast ? " a voice comes musically.
Mirèio's.   Vincen darts beneath the trees,
Looks up, and soon the merry maiden sees.

Perched on a mulberry-tree, she eyed the la
Like some gray-crested lark, and he was glad.

" How then, Mirèio, comes the picking on ?
Little by little, all will soon be done !
May I not help thee ?"—" That were very meet,"
She said, and laughed upon her airy seat.
Sprang Vincen like a squirrel from the clover,
Ran nimbly up the tree, and said, moreover—

"Now since old Master Ramoun hath but thee,
Come down, I pray, and strip the lower tree !
I'll to the top !"   As busily the maiden
Wrought on, she   murmured,   " How   the   soul   doth
    gladden
To have good company !   There's little joy
In lonely work !"—" Ay is there !" said the boy :

" For when in our old hut we sit alone,
Father and I, and only hear the Rhone
Rush headlong o'er the shingle, 'tis most drear !
Not in the pleasant season of the year,
For then upon our travels we are bound,
And trudge from farm to farm the country round.

" But when the holly-berries have turned red,
And winter comes, and nights are long," he said,
" And sitting by the dying fire we catch
Whistle or mew of goblin at the latch ;
And I must wait till bed-time there with him,
Speaking but seldom, and the room so dim,"—

Broke in the happy girl, unthinkingly,
" Ah ! but your mother, Vincen, where is she ?"
" Mother is dead."   The two were still awhile :
Then he, " But Vinceneto could beguile
The time when she was there.   A little thing,
But she could keep the hut."—" I'm wondering—

"You have a sister, Vincen ? "—" That have I !
A merry lass and good," was the reply :
" For down at Font-dou-Rèi, in Beaucaire,
Whither she went to glean, she was so fair
And deft at work that all were smitten by her ;
And there she stays as servant by desire."

"And you are like her ? "—"Now that makes me merry.
Why, she is blonde, and I brown as a berry !
But wouldst thou know whom she is like, the elf ?
Why, even like thee, Mirèio, thine own self !
Your two bright heads, with all their wealth of hair
Like myrtle-leaves, would make a perfect pair.

" But, ah ! thou knowest better far to gather
The muslin of thy cap than doth the other !
My little sister is not plain nor dull,
But thou,—thou art so much more beautiful !"
" Oh, what a Vincen ! " cried Mirèio,
And suddenly the half-culled branch let go.

Sing, magnarello, merrily,
    As the green leaves you gather !
In their third sleep the silk-worms lie,
    And lovely is the weather.
Like brown bees that in open glades
    From rosemary gather honey,
The mulberry-trees swarm full of maids,
    Glad as the air is sunny !

"And so you fancy I am fair to view,
Fairer than Vinceneto ? "   " That I do ! "
"But what advantage have I more than she ? "
" Mother divine ! " he cried, impetuously,
"That of the goldfinch o'er the fragile wren—
Grace for the eye—song for the hearts of men

"What more? Ah, my poor sister! Hear me speak,—
Thou wilt not get the white out of the leek:
Her eyes are like the water of the sea,
Blue, clear—thine, black, and they flash gloriously.
And, O Mirèio! when on me they shine,
I seem to drain a bumper of cooked wine!

"My sister hath a silver voice and mellow,—
I love to hear her sing the *Peirounello*,—
But, ah! my sweet young lady, every word
Thou'st given me my spirit more hath stirred,
My ear more thrilled, my very heart-strings wrung,
More than a thousand songs divinely sung!

"With roaming all the pastures in the sun,
My little sister's face and neck are dun
As dates; but thou, most fair one, I think well,
Art fashioned like the flowers of Asphodel.
So the bold Summer with his tawny hand
Dare not caress thy forehead white and bland.

"Moreover, Vinceneto is more slim
Than dragon-flies that o'er the brooklet skim.
Poor child! In one year grew she up to this;
But verily in thy shape is naught amiss."
Again Mirèio, turning rosy red,
Let fall her branch, and "What a Vincen!" said.

Sing, magnarello, merrily,
  The green leaves ever piling!
Two comely children sit on high,
  Amid the foliage, smiling.
Sing, magnarello, loud and oft:
  Your merry labour hasten.
The guileless pair who laugh aloft
  Are learning love's first lesson.

Cleared from the hills meanwhile the mists of morn,
And o'er the ruined towers, whither return
Nightly the grim old lords of Baux, they say;
And o'er the barren rocks 'gan take their way
Vultures, whose large, white wings are seen to gleam
Resplendent in the noontide's burning beam.

Then cried the maiden, pouting, "We have done
Naught! Oh, shame to idle so! *Some one*
Said he would help me; and that some one still
Doth naught but talk, and make me laugh at will.
Work now, lest mother say I am unwary
And idle, and too awkward yet to marry!

"Ah! my brave friend, I think should one engage you
To pick leaves by the quintal, and for wage, you
Would all the same sit still and feast your eyes,
Handling the ready sprays in dreamy wise!"
Whereat the boy, a trifle disconcerted,
"And so thou takest me for a gawky!" blurted.

"We'll see, my fair young lady," added he,
"Which of us two the better picker be!"
They ply both hands now. With vast animation,
They bend and strip the branches. No occasion
For rest or idle chatter either uses
(The bleating sheep, they say, her mouthful loses),

Until the mulberry-tree is bare of leaves,
And these the ready sack at once receives,
At whose distended mouth—ah, youth is sweet!—
Mirèio's pretty taper hand will meet
In strange entanglement that somehow lingers
That Vincen's, with its brown and burning fingers.

Both started. In their cheeks the flush rose higher;
They felt the heat of some mysterious fire.

They dropped the mulberry-leaves as if afraid,
And, tremulous with passion, the boy said,—
"What aileth thee, my lady? answer me!
Did any hidden hornet dare sting thee?"

Well-nigh inaudible, with head bent low,
"I know not, Vincen,"—thus Mirèio.
And so they turned a few more leaves to gather,
And for a while spake not again, but rather
Exchanged bright looks and sidelong, saying well
The one who first should laugh, would break the spell.

Their hearts beat high, the green leaves fell like rain;
And, when the time for sacking came again,
Whether by chance or by contrivance, yet
The white hand and the brown hand always met.
Nor seemed there any lack of happiness
The while their labour failed not to progress.

　　　Sing, magnarello, merrily,
　　　　　As the green leaves you gather!
　　　The sun of May is riding high,
　　　　　And ardent is the weather.

Now suddenly Mirèio whispered, "Hark!
What can that be?" and listened like a lark
Upon a vine, her small forefinger pressing
Against her lip, and eager eyes addressing
To a bird's nest upon a leafy bough,
Just opposite the one where she was now.

"Ah! wait a little while!" with bated breath,
So the young basket-weaver answereth,
And like a sparrow hopped from limb to limb
Toward the nest. Down in the tree-trunk dim,
Close peering through a crevice in the wood,
Full-fledged and lively saw he the young brood.

And, sitting firmly the rough bough astride,
Clung with one hand, and let the other glide
Into the hollow trunk.   Above his head
Mirèio leaned with her cheeks rosy red.
"What sort?" she whispered from her covert shady.
"Beauties!"—"But what?"—"Blue tomtits, my young
    lady!"

Then laughed the maiden, and her laugh was gay:
"See, Vincen!   Have you never heard them say
That when two find a nest in company,
On mulberry, or any other tree,
The Church within a year will join those two?
And proverbs, father says, are always true."

"Yea," quoth the lad; "but do not thou forget
That this, our happy hope, may perish yet,
If all the birdies be not caged forthwith."
"Jesu divine!" the maiden murmureth:
"Put them by quickly!   It concerns us much
Our birdies should be safe from alien touch."

"Why, then, the very safest place," said he,
"Methinks, Mirèio, would thy bodice be!"
"Oh, surely!"   So the lad explores the hollow,
His hand withdrawing full of tomtits callow.
Four were they; and the maid in ecstacy
Cries "Mon Dieu!" and lifts her hands on high.

"How many!   What a pretty brood it is!
There!   There, poor darlings, give me just one kiss!"
And, lavishing a thousand fond caresses,
Tenderly, carefully, the four she presses
Inside her waist, obeying Vincen's will;
While he, "Hold out thy hands! there are more still!"

"Oh sweet!   The little eyes in each blue head
Are sharp as needles," as Mirèio said

Softly, three more of the wee brood she pressed
Into their smooth, white prison with the rest,
Who, when bestowed within that refuge warm,
Thought they were in their nest and safe from harm.

" Are there more, Vincen? "—" Ay ! " he answered her.
" Then, Holy Virgin ! you're a sorcerer ! "
" Thou simple maid !   About St. George's day,
Ten, twelve, and fourteen eggs, these tomtits lay.
Ay, often.   Now let these the others follow !
They are the last : so good-bye, pretty hollow ! "

But ere the words were spoken, and the maid
In her flowered neckerchief had fairly laid
Her little charge, she gave a piercing wail :
" Oh me ! oh me ! " then murmured, and turned pale ;
And, laying both her hands upon her breast,
Moaned, " I am dying ! " and was sore distressed,

And could but weep : " Ah, they are scratching me !
They sting !   Come quickly, Vincent, up the tree ! "
For on the last arrival had ensued
Wondrous commotion in the hidden brood ;
The fledglings latest taken from the nest
Had sore disorder wrought among the rest.

Because within so very small a valley
All could not lie at ease, so must they gayly
Scramble with claw and wing down either slope,
And up the gentle hills, thus to find scope :
A thousand tiny somersets they turn,
A thousand pretty rolls they seem to learn.

And " Ah, come quick ! " is still the maiden's cry,
Trembling like vine-spray when the wind is high,
Or like a heifer stung with cattle-flies.
And, as she bends and writhes in piteous wise,
Leaps Vincen upward till he plants his feet
Once more beside her on her airy seat.

Sing, magnarello, heap your leaves,
   While sunny is the weather !
He comes to aid her when she grieves :
   The two are now together.

"' Thou likest not this tickling ?" kindly said he.
"' What if thou wert like me, my gentle lady,
And hadst to wander barefoot through the nettles ?"
So proffering his red sea-cap, there he settles
Fast as she draws them from her neckerchief
The birdies, to Mirèio's vast relief.

Yet ah, poor dear, the downcast eyes of her !
She dares not look at her deliverer
For a brief space.   But soon a smile ensues,
And the tears vanish, as the morning dews
That drench the flowers and grass at break of day
Roll into little pearls and pass away.

And then there came a fresh catastrophe :
The branch whereon they sat ensconced in glee
Snapped, broke asunder, and with ringing shriek
Mirèio flung her arms round Vincen's neck,
And he clasped hers, and they whirled suddenly
Down through the leaves upon the supple rye.

Listen, wind of the Greek, wind of the sea,
And shake no more the verdant canopy !
Hush for one moment, O thou childish breeze !
Breathe soft and whisper low, beholding these !
Give them a little time to dream of bliss,—
To dream at least, in such a world as this !

Thou too, swift streamlet of the prattling voice,
Peace, prithee !   In this hour, make little noise
Among the vocal pebbles of thy bed !
Ay, little noise !   Because two souls have sped
To one bright region.   Leave them there, to roam
Over the starry heights,—their proper home !

A moment, and she struggled to be free
From his embrace.   The flower of the quince-tree
Is not so pale.   Then backward the two sank,
And gazed at one another on the bank,
Until the weaver's son the silence brake,
And thus in seeming wrath arose and spake :

"Shame on thee, thou perfidious mulberry !
A devil's tree !   A Friday-planted tree !
Blight seize and wood-louse eat thee !   May thy master
Hold thee in horror for this day's disaster !
Tell me thou art not hurt, Mirèio !"
Trembling from head to foot, she answered, " No :

" I am not hurt ; but as a baby weeps
And knows not why,—there's something here that keeps
Perpetual tumult in my heart.   A pain
Blinds me and deafens me, and fills my brain,
So that my blood in a tumultuous riot
Courses my body through, and won't be quiet."

"May it not be," the simple boy replied,
"Thou fearest to have thy mother come and chide
Thy tardy picking,—as when I come back
Late from the blackberry-field with face all black,
And tattered clothes ? "   Mirèio sighed again,
" Ah, no !   This is another kind of pain !"

"Or possibly a sun-stroke may have lighted
Upon thee ! "   And the eager Vincen cited
An ancient crone among the hills of Baux,
Taven by name, "who on the forehead,—so,—
A glass of water sets : the ray malign
The dazed brain for the crystal will resign."

"Nay, nay ! " impetuously the maiden cried,
"Floods of May sunshine never terrified

The girls of Crau. Why should I hold you waiting?
Vincen, in vain my heart is palpitating !
My secret cannot bide a home so small :
I love you, Vincen, love you !—That is all ! "

The river-banks, the close-pruned willows hoary,
Green grass and ambient air, hearing this story,
Were full of glee. But the poor basket-weaver,
" Princess, that thou who art so fair and clever,
Shouldst have a tongue given to wicked lying !
Why, it confounds me ! It is stupefying !

" What ! thou in love with me ? Mirèio,
My poor life is yet happy. Do not go
And make a jest thereof ! I might believe
Just for one moment, and thereafter grieve
My soul to death. Ah, no ! my pretty maid,
Laugh no more at me in this wise ! " he said.

" Now may God shut me out of Paradise,
Vincen, if I have ever told you lies !
Go to ! I love you ! Will that kill you, friend ?
But if you *will* be cruel, and so send
Me from your side, 'tis I who will fall ill,
And at your feet lie low till sorrow kill ! "

" No more ! no more ! " cried Vincen, desperately :
" There is a gulf 'twixt thee and me ! The stately
Queen of the Lotus Farm art thou, and all
Bow at thy coming, hasten to thy call,
While I, a vagrant weaver, only wander,
Plying my trade from Valabrègo yonder."

" What care I ? " cried the fiery girl at once.
Sharp as a sheaf-binder's came her response.
" May not my lover, then, a baron be,
Or eke a weaver, if he pleases me ?
But if you will not have me pine away,
Why look so handsome, even in rags, I say?"

He turned and faced her.   Ah, she was enchanting !
And as a charmèd bird falls dizzy, panting,
So he.   " Mirèio, thou'rt a sorceress !
And I bedazzled by thy loveliness.
Thy voice, too, mounts into this head of mine,
And makes me like a man o'ercome with wine.

" Why, can it be, Mirèio?   Seest thou not
Even now with thy embrace my brain is hot.
I am a pack-bearer, and well may be
A laughing-stock for evermore to thee,
But thou shalt have the truth, dear, in this hour :
I love thee, with a love that could devour !

" Wert thou to ask,—lo, love I thee so much !—
The golden goat, that ne'er felt mortal touch
Upon its udders, but doth only lick
Moss from the base of the precipitous peak
Of Baux,—I'd perish in the quarries there,
Or bring thee down the goat with golden hair !

" So much, that, if thou saidst, ' I want a star,'
There is no stream so wild, no sea so far,
But I would cross ; no headsman, steel or fire,
That could withhold me.   Yea, I would climb higher
Than peaks that kiss the sky, that star to wrest ;
And Sunday thou shouldst wear it on thy breast !

" O my Mirèio !   Ever as I gaze,
Thy beauty fills me with a deep amaze.
Once, when by Vaucluse grotto I was going,
I saw a fig-tree in the bare rock growing ;
So very spare it was, the lizards gray
Had found more shade beneath a jasmine spray.

" But, round about the roots, once every year
The neighbouring stream comes gushing, as I hear,

And the shrub drinks the water as it rises,
And that one drink for the whole year suffices.
Even as the gem is cut to fit the ring,
This parable to us is answering.

" I am the fig-tree on the barren mountain ;
And thou, mine own, art the reviving fountain !
Surely it would suffice me, could I feel
That, once a year, I might before thee kneel,
And sun myself in thy sweet face, and lay
My lips unto thy fingers, as to-day ! "

Trembling with love, Mirèio hears him out,
And lets him wind his arms her neck about
And clasp her as bewildered.   Suddenly,
Through the green walk, quavers an old wife's cry :
" How now, Mirèio ?   Are you coming soon ?
What will the silk-worms have to eat at noon ? "

As ofttimes, at the coming on of night,
A flock of sparrows on a pine alight
And fill the air with joyous chirruping,
Yet, if a passing gleaner pause and fling
A stone that way, they to the neighbouring wood,
By terror winged, their instant flight make good ;

So, with a tumult of emotion thrilled,
Fled the enamoured two across the field.
But when, her leaves upon her head, the maid
Turned silently toward the farm, he stayed,—
Vincen,—and breathless watched her in her flight
Over the fallow, till she passed from sight.

CANTO III.

The Cocooning.

WHEN the crop is fair in the olive-yard,
　　And the earthen jars are ready
For the golden oil from the barrels poured,
　　And the big cart rocks unsteady
With its tower of gathered sheaves, and strains
And groans on its way through fields and lanes ;

When brawny and bare as an old athlete
　　Comes Bacchus the dance a-leading,
And the labourers all, with juice-dyed feet,
　　The vintage of Crau are treading,
And the good wine pours from the brimful presses,
And the ruddy foam in the vats increases ;

When under the leaves of the Spanish broom
　　The clear silk-worms are holden,
An artist each, in a tiny loom,
　　Weaving a web all golden,—
Fine, frail cells out of sunlight spun,
Where they creep and sleep by the million,—

Glad is Provence on a day like that,
　　'Tis the time of jest and laughter :
The Ferigoulet and the Baume Muscat
　　They quaff, and they sing thereafter.
And lads and lasses, their toils between,
Dance to the tinkling tambourine.

" Methinks, good neighbours, I am Fortune's pet.
Ne'er in my trellised arbor saw I yet
A silkier bower, cocoons more worthy praise,
Or richer harvest, since the year of grace
When first I laid my hand on Ramoun's arm
And came, a youthful bride, to Lotus Farm."

So spake Jano Mario, Ramoun's wife,
The fond, proud mother who had given life
To our Mirèio. Unto her had hied,
The while were gathered the cocoons outside,
Her neighbours. In the silk-worm-room they throng ;
And, as they aid the picking, gossip long.

To these Mirèio tendered now and then
Oak-sprigs and sprays of rosemary ; for when
The worms, lured by the mountain odour, come
In myriads, there to make their silken home,
The sprays and sprigs, adornèd in such wise,
Are like the golden palms of Paradise.

" On Mother Mary's altar yesterday,"
Jano Mario said, " I went to lay
My finer sprays, by way of tithe.   And so
I do each year ; for you, my women, know
That, when the holy Mother will, 'tis she
Who sendeth up the worms abundantly."

" Now, for my part," said Zèu of Host Farm,
" Great fears have I my worms will come to harm.
You mind that ugly day the east wind blew,—
I left my window open,—if you knew
Ever such folly !—and to my affright
Upon my floor are twenty, now turned white."

To Zèu thus the crone Taven replied—
A witch, who from the cliffs of Baux had hied

To help at the cocooning : " Youth is bold,
The young think they know better than the old ;
And age is torment, and we mourn the fate
Which bids us see and know,—but all too late,

" Ye are such giddy women, every one,
That, if the hatching promise well, ye run
Straightway about the streets the tale to tell.
' Come see my silk-worms !   'Tis incredible
How fine they are ! "   Envy can well dissemble :
She hastens to your room, her heart a-tremble

" With wrath.   And 'Well done, neighbour !' she says cheerly :
'This does one good ! You've still your caul on, clearly !'
But when your head is turned, she casts upon 'em—
The envious one—a look so full of venom,
It knots and burns 'em up.   And then you say
It was the east wind plastered 'em that way ! "

" I don't say that has naught to do with it,"
Quoth Zèu.   " Still it had been quite as fit
For me to close the window."—" Doubt you, then,
The harm the eye can do," went on Taven,
" When in the head it glistens balefully ? "
And Zèu scanned, herself with piercing eye.

" Ye are such fools, ye seem to think," she said,
" That scraping with a scalpel on the dead
Would win its honey-secret from the bee !
But may not a fierce look, now answer me,
The unborn babe for evermore deform,
And dry the cow's milk in her udders warm ?

" An owl may fascinate a little bird ;
A serpent, flying geese, as I have heard,

How high soe'er they mount.   And if one keep
A fixed gaze upon silk-worms, will they sleep?
Moreover, is there, neighbours, in the land
So wise a virgin that she can withstand

"The fiery eyes of passionate youth?"   Here stopped
The hag, and damsels four their cocoons dropped;
"In June as in October," murmuring,
"Her tongue hath evermore a barbèd sting,
The ancient viper!   What! the lads, say you?
Let them come, then!   We'll see what they can do?"

But other merry ones retorted, "No!
We want them not!   Do we, Mirèio?"
"Not we!   Nor is it always cocooning,
So I'll a bottle from the cellar bring
That you will find delicious."   And she fled
Toward the house because her cheeks grew red.

"Now, friends," said haughty Lauro, with decision,
"This is my mind, though poor be my condition:
I'll smile on no one, even though my lover
As king of fairy-land his realm should offer.
A pleasure were it, could I see him lying,
And seven long years before my footstool sighing."

"Ah!" said Clemenço, "should a king me woo,
And say he loved me, without much ado
I'd grant the royal suit!   And chiefly thus
Were he a young king and a glorious.
A king of men, in beauty, I'd let come
And freely lead me to his palace home!

"But see!   If I were once enthronèd there,
A sovereign and an empress, in a fair
Mantle bedecked, of golden-flowered brocade,
With pearls and emeralds dazzling round my head,
Then would my heart for my poor country yearn;
And I, the queen, would unto Baux return.

" And I would make my capital at Baux,
And on the rock where lie its ruins low
I would rebuild our ancient castle, and
A white tower on the top thereof should stand
Whose head should touch the stars.   Thither retiring,
If rest or solace were the queen desiring,

" We'd climb the turret-stair, my prince and I,
And gladly throw the crown and mantle by.
And would it not be blissful with my love,
Aloft, alone to sit, the world above ?
Or, leaned upon the parapet by his side,
To search the lovely landscape far and wide,

"Our own glad kingdom of Provence descrying,
Like some great orange-grove beneath us lying
All fair ?   And, ever stretching dreamily
Beyond the hills and plains, the sapphire sea ;
While noble ships, tricked out with streamers gay,
Just graze the Chateau d'If, and pass away?

" Or we would turn to lightning-scathed Ventour,
Who, while the lesser heights before him cower,
His hoary head against the heaven raises,
As I have seen, in solitary places
Of beech and pine, with staff in agèd hand,
Some shepherd-chief, his flock o'erlooking, stand.

" Again, we'd follow the great Rhone awhile,
Adown whose banks the cities brave defile,
And dip their lips and drink, with dance and song.
Stately is the Rhone's march, and very strong ;
But even he must bend at Avignon
His haughty head to Notre Dame des Doms.

"Or watch the ever-varying Durance,
Now like some fierce and ravenous goat advance

Devouring banks and bridges ; now demure
As maid from rustic well who bears her ewer,
Spilling her scanty water as she dallies,
And every youth along her pathway rallies.'

So spake her sweet Provençal majesty,
And rose with brimful apron, and put by
Her gathered treasure.   Two more maids were there,
Twin sisters, the one dark, the other fair,—
Azaläis, Viòulano.   The stronghold
Of Estoublon sheltered their parents old.

And oft these two to Lotus Farmstead came :
While that mischievous lad, Cupid by name,
Who loves to sport with generous hearts and tender,
Had made the sisters both their love surrender
To the same youth.   So Azaläis said,—
The dark one,—lifting up her raven head :

"Now, damsels, play awhile that I were queen.
The Marseilles ships, the Beaucaire meadows green,
Smiling La Ciotat, and fair Salon,
With all her almond trees, to me belong.
Then the young maids I'd summon by decree,
From Arles, Baux, Barbentano, unto me.

" 'Come, fly like birds !' the order should be given ;
And I, of these, would choose the fairest seven,
And royal charge upon the same would lay,
The false love and the true in scales to weigh.
And then would merry counsel holden be ;
For sure it is a great calamity

" That half of those who love, with love most meet,
Can never marry, and their joy complete.
But when I, Azaläis, hold the helm,
I proclamation make, that in my realm
True lovers wounded in their cruel sport
Shall aye find mercy at the maiden's court.

" And if one sell her robe of honour white,
Whether it be for gold or jewel bright,
And if one offer insult, or betray
A fond heart, unto such as these alway
The high court of the seven maids shall prove
The stern avenger of offended love.

" And if two lovers the same maid desire,
Or if two maids to the same lad aspire,
My council's duty it shall be to choose
Which loves the better, which the better sues,
And which is worthier of a happy fate.
Moreover, on my maidens there shall wait

"Seven sweet poets, who from time to time
Shall write the laws of love in lovely rhyme
Upon wild vine-leaves or the bark of trees ;
And sometimes, in a stately chorus, these
Will sing the same, and then their couplets all
Like honey from the honey-comb will fall."

So, long ago, the whispering pines among,
Faneto de Gautèume may have sung,
When she the glory of her star-crowned head
On Roumanin and on the Alpines shed ;
Or Countess Dio, of the passionate lays,
Who held her courts of love in the old days.

But now Mirèio, to the room returning,
With face as radiant as an Easter morning,
A flagon bore ; and, for their spirits' sake,
Besought them all her beverage to partake :
" For this will make us work with heartier will ;
So come, good women, and your goblets fill ! "

Then, pouring from the wicker-covered flask
A generous drink for whosoe'er might ask,

(A string of gold the falling liquor made),
" I mixed this cordial mine own self," she said :
"One leaves it in a window forty days,
That it may mellow in the sun's hot rays.

" Herein are mountain herbs, in number three.
The liquor keeps their odour perfectly :
It strengthens one."   Here brake in other voices:
" Listen, Mirèio !   Tell us what your choice is ;
For these have told what they would do, if they
Were queens, or came to great estate one day.

" In such a case, Mirèio, what would you ? "
" Who, I ?   How can I tell what I would do ?
I am so happy in our own La Crau
With my dear parents, wherefore should I go ? "
" Ah, ha ! " outspake another maiden bold :
" Little care you for silver or for gold.

" But on a certain morn, I mind it well,—
Forgive me, dear, that I the tale should tell !—
'Twas Tuesday : I had gathered sticks that day,
And, fagot on my hip, had won my way
Almost to La Crous-Blanco, when I 'spied
You in a tree, with some one by your side

" Who chatted gayly.   A lithe form he had "—
" Whence did he come ? " they cried.   " Who was the
    lad ? "
Said Noro, " To tell that were not so easy,
Because among the thick-leaved mulberry-trees he
Was hidden half; yet think I 'twas the clever
Vincen, the Valabregan basket-weaver ! "

" Oh ! " cried the damsels all, with peals of laughter,
" See you not what the little cheat was after ?
A pretty basket she would fain receive,
And made this poor boy in her love believe !
The fairest maiden the whole country over
Has chosen the barefoot Vincen for her lover ! "
c*

So mocked they, till o'er each young countenance
In turn there fell a dark and sidelong glance,—
Taven's,—who cried, "A thousand curses fall
Upon you, and the vampire seize you all!
If the good Lord from heaven this way came,
You girls, I think, would giggle all the same.

" 'Tis brave to laugh at this poor lad of osiers ;
But mark ! the future may make strange disclosures,
Poor though he be.   Now hear the oracle !
God in his house once wrought a miracle ;
And I can show the truth of what I say,
For, lasses, it all happened in my day.

" Once, in the wild woods of the Luberon,
A shepherd kept his flock.   His days were long ;
But when at last the same were well-nigh spent,
And toward the grave his iron frame was bent,
He sought the hermit of Saint Ouquèri,
To make his last confession piously.

" Alone, in the Vaumasco valley lost,
His foot had never sacred threshold crost,
Since he partook his first communion.
Even his prayers were from his memory gone ;
But now he rose and left his cottage lowly,
And came and bowed before the hermit holy.

" ' With what sin chargest thou thyself, my brother?'
The solitary said.   Replied the other,
The aged man, ' Once, long ago, I slew
A little bird about my flock that flew,—
A cruel stone I flung its life to end :
It was a wagtail, and the shepherds' friend.

" ' Is this a simple soul,' the hermit thought,
' Or is it an impostor?'   And he sought

Right curiously to read the old man's face
Until, to solve the riddle, ' Go,' he says,
' And hang thy shepherd's cloak yon beam upon,
And afterward I will absolve my son.'

" A single sunbeam through the chapel strayed ;
And there it was the priest the suppliant bade
To hang his cloak !   But the good soul arose,
And drew it off with mien of all repose,
And threw it upward.   And it hung in sight
Suspended on the slender shaft of light !

" Then fell the hermit prostrate on the floor,
' Oh, man of God ! ' he cried, and he wept sore,
' Let but the blessed hand these tears bedew,
Fulfil the sacred office for us two !
No sins of thine can I absolve, 'tis clear :
Thou art the saint, and I the sinner here ! ' "

Her story ended, the crone said no more ;
But all the laughter of the maids was o'er.
Only Laureto dared one little joke :
" This tells us ne'er to laugh at any cloak !
Good may the beast be, although rough the hide ;
But, girls, methought young mistress I espied

" Grow crimson as an autumn grape, because
Vincen's dear name so lightly uttered was.
There's mystery here !   Mirèio, we are jealous !
Lasted the picking long that day?   Pray, tell us !
When two friends meet, the hour is winged with pleasure ;
And, for a lover, one has always leisure ! "

" Oh, fie ! " Mirèio said.   " Enough of joking !
Mind your work now, and be not so provoking !
You would make swear the very saints !   But I
Promise you one and all, most faithfully,
I'll seek a convent while my years are tender,
Sooner than e'er my maiden heart surrender ! '

Then brake the damsels into merry chorus:
" Have we not pretty Magali before us?
Who love and lovers held in such disdain
That, to escape their torment, she was fain
To Saint Blasi's in Arles away to hie,
And bury her sweet self from every eye."

" Come, Noro, you, whose voice is ever thrilling,
Who charm us all, sing now, if you are willing,
The song of Magali, the cunning fairy,
Who love had shunned by all devices airy.
A bird, a vine, a sunbeam she became,
Yet fell herself, love's victim all the same !

" Queen of my soul ! " sang Noro, and the rest
Fell straightway to their work with twofold zest ;
And as, when one cicala doth begin
Its high midsummer note, the rest fall in
And swell the chorus, so the damsels here
Sang the refrain with voices loud and clear :—

I.

" Magali, queen of my soul,
   The dawn is near !
Hark to my tambourine,
Hide not thy bower within,
   Open and hear !

II.

" The sky is full of stars,
   And the wind soft ;
But, when thine eyes they see,
The stars, O Magali,
   Will pale aloft ! "

III.

" Idle as summer breeze
 The tune thou playest !
I'll vanish in the sea,
A silver eel will be,
 Ere thou me stayest."

IV.

" If thou become an eel,
 And so forsake me,
I will turn fisher boy,
And fish the water blue
 Until I take thee !"

.V.

" In vain with net or line
 Thou me implorest :
I'll be a bird that day,
And wing my trackless way
 Into the forest !"

VI.

" If thou become a bird,
 And so dost dare me,
I will a fowler be,
And follow cunningly
 Until I snare thee !"

VII.

" When thou thy cruel snare
 Settest full surely,
I will a flower become,
And in my prairie home
 Hide me securely !"

VIII.

" If thou become a flower,
    Before thou thinkest
I'll be a streamlet clear,
And all the water bear
    That thou, love, drinkest ! "

IX.

"When thou, a stream, dost feed
    The flower yonder,
I will turn cloud straightway,
And to America
    Away I'll wander."

X.

" Though thou to India
    Fly from thy lover,
Still I will follow thee :
I the sea-breeze will be
    To waft thee over ! "

XI.

" I can outstrip the breeze
    Fast as it flieth :
I'll be the swift sun-ray
That melts the ice away
    And the grass drieth ! "

XII.

" Sunlight if thou become,
    Are my wiles ended ?
I'll be a lizard green,
And quaff the golden sheen
    To make me splendid ! "

XIII.

" Be thou a Triton, hid
  In the dark sedges !
I'm the moon by whose ray
Fairies and witches pay
  Their mystic pledges ! "

XIV.

" If thou the moon wilt be
  Sailing in glory,
I'll be the halo white
Hovering every night
  Around and o'er thee ! "

XV.

" Yet shall thy shadowy arm
  Embrace me never !
I will turn virgin rose,
And all my thorns oppose
  To thee for ever ! "

XVI.

" If thou become a rose,
  Vain too shall this be !
Seest thou not that I,
As a bright butterfly,
  Freely may kiss thee ? "

XVII.

" Urge, then, thy mad pursuit :
  Idly thou'lt follow !
I'll in the deep wood bide ;
I'll in the old oak hide,
  Gnarlèd and hollow."

XVIII.

"In the dim forest glade
  Wilt thou be hidden?
I'll be the ivy-vine,
And my long arms entwine
  Round thee unbidden!"

XIX.'

" Fold thine arms tightly, then :
  Clasp the oak only!
I'll a white sister be!
Far off in St. Blasi,
  Secure and lonely!"

XX.

" Be thou a white-veiled nun
  Come to confession,
I will be there as priest,
Thee freely to divest
  Of all transgression!"

The startled women their cocoons let fall.
"Noro, make haste!" outspake they one and all:
"What could our hunted Magali answer then?
A nun, poor dear, who had already been
A cloud, a bird, a fish, an oak, a flower,
The sun, the moon, the stream, in one short hour?"

" Ah, yes!" said Noro, " I the rest will sing:
She was, I think, the cloister entering;
And that mad fowler dared to promise her
He would in the confessional appear,
And shrive her.   Therefore hear what she replies:
The maid hath yet another last device:"—

XXI.

" Enter the sacred house !
I shall be sleeping,
Robed in a winding-sheet,
Nuns at my head and feet,
Above me weeping."

XXII.

" If thou wert lifeless dust,
My toils were o'er :
I'd be the yawning grave,
Thee in my arms to have
For evermore ! "

XXIII.

" Now know I thou art true,
Leave me not yet !
Come, singer fair, and take,
And wear it for my sake,
This annulet ! "

XXIV.

" Look up, my blessed one,
The heaven scan !
Since the stars came to see
Thee, O my Magali,
They are turned wan ! ".

A silence fell, the sweet song being ended :
Only with the last moving notes had blended
The voices of the rest.   Their heads were drooping,
As they before the melody were stooping,
Like slender reeds that lean and sway for ever
Before the flowing eddies of a river.

Till Noro said, " Now is the air serene ;
And here the mowers come, their scythes to clean
Beside the vivary brook.　Mirèio, dear,
Bring us a few St. John's Day apples here.
And we will add a little new-made cheese,
And take our lunch beneath the lotus-trees."

CANTO IV.

The Suitors.

WHEN violets are blue in the blue shadows
  Of the o'erhanging trees,
The youth who stray in pairs about the meadows
  Are glad to gather these.

When peace descends upon the troubled Ocean,
  And he his wrath forgets,
Flock from Martigue the boats with wing-like motion,
  The fishes fill their nets.

And when the girls of Crau bloom into beauty
  (And fairer earth knows not),
Aye are there suitors ready for their duty
  In castle and in cot.

Thus to Mirèio's home came seeking her
A trio notable,—a horse-tamer,
A herdsman, and a shepherd.   It befell
The last was first who came his tale to tell.
Alari was his name, a wealthy man,—
He had a thousand sheep, the story ran.

The same were wont to feed the winter long
In rich salt-pastures by Lake Entressen.
And at wheat-bolling time, in burning May,
Himself would often lead his flock, they say,
Up through the hills to pastures green and high :
They say moreover, and full faith have I,

That ever as St. Mark's came round again
Nine noted shearers Alari would retain
Three days to shear his flock.   Added to these
A man to bear away each heavy fleece,
And a sheep-boy who back and forward ran
And filled the shearer's quickly emptied can.

But when the summer heats began to fail
And the high peaks to feel the snowy gale,
A stately sight it was that flock to see
Wind from the upper vales of Dauphiny,
And o'er the Crau pursue their devious ways,
Upon the toothsome winter grass to graze.

Also to watch them there where they defile
Into the stony road were well worth while ;
The early lambkins all the rest outstripping
And merrily about the lamb-herd leaping,
The bell-decked asses with their foals beside,
Or following after them.   These had for guide

A drover, who a patient mule bestrode.
Its wattled panniers bare a motley load :
Food for the shepherd-folk, and flasks of wine,
And the still bleeding hides of slaughtered kine ;
And folded garments whereon oft there lay
Some weakly lamb, a-weary of the way.

Next came abreast—the captains of the host—
Five fiery bucks, their fearsome heads uptost :
With bells loud jingling and with sidelong glances,
And backward curving horns, each one advances.
The sober mothers follow close behind,
Striving their lawless little kids to mind.

A rude troop and a ravenous they are,
And these the goat-herd hath in anxious care.

And after them there follow presently
The great ram-chiefs, with muzzles lifted high :
You know them by the heavy horn that lies
Thrice curved about the ear in curious wise.

Their ribs and backs with tufts of wool are decked,
That they may have their meed of due respect
As the flock's grandsires.   Plain to all beholders,
With sheepskin cloak folded about his shoulders,
Strides the chief-shepherd next, with lordly swing ;
The main corps of his army following.

Tumbling through clouds of dust, the great ewe-dams
Call with loud bleatings to their bleating lambs.
The little hornèd ones are gayly drest,
With tiny tufts of scarlet on the breast
And o'er the neck.   While, filling the next place,
The woolly sheep advance at solemn pace.

Amid the tumult now and then the cries
Of shepherd-boy to shepherd-dog arise.
For now the pitch-marked herd innumerable
Press forward : yearlings, two-year-olds as well,
Those who have lost their lambs, and those who bear
Twin lambs unborn,—and wearily they fare.

A ragamuffin troop brings up the rear.
The barren and past-breeding ewes are here,
The lame, the toothless, and the remnant sorry
Of many a mighty ram, lean now and hoary,
Who from his earthly labours long hath rested,
Of honour and of horns alike divested.

All these who fill the road and mountain-passes—
Old, young, good, bad, and neither ; sheep, goats, asses—
Are Alari's, every one.   He stands the while
And watches them, a hundred in a file,
Pass on before him ; and the man's eyes laugh.
His wand of office is a maple staff.

And when to pasture with his dogs hies he,
And leathern gaiters buttoned to the knee,
His forehead to an ample wisdom grown
And air serene might be King David's own,
When in his youth he led, as the tale tells,
The flocks at eve beside his father's wells.

This was the chief toward Lotus Farm who drew,
And presently Mirèio's self who knew
Flitting about the doorway.   His heart bounded.
"Good Heaven !" he cried, "her praises they have
    sounded
Nowise too loudly ! Ne'er saw I such grace
Or high or low, in life or pictured face !"

Only that face to see, his flock forsaking,
Alari had come.   Yet now his heart was quaking
When, standing in the presence of the maid,
"Would you so gracious be, fair one," he said,
"As to point out the way these hills to cross?
For else find I myself at utter loss."

"Oh, yes !" replied the girl, ingenuously,
"Thou takest the straight road, and comest thereby
Into Pèiro-malo desert.   Then
Follow the winding path till thou attain
A portico with an old tomb anear :
Two statues of great generals it doth bear.

Antiquities they call them hereabout."
"Thanks, many !" said the youth.   "I had come out
A thousand of my woolly tribe, or so,
To lead into the mountains from La Crau.
We leave to-morrow.   I their way direct,
And sleeping-spots and feeding-ground select.

"They bear my mark, and are of fine breed, all ;
And for my shepherdess, when one I call

My own, the nightingales will ever sing.
And dared I hope you'd take my offering,
Mirèio dear, no gems I'd tender you,
But a carved box-wood cup,—mine own work too!"

Therewith he brought to light a goblet fair,
Wrapped like some sacred relic with all care,
And carven of box-wood green. It was his pleasure
Such things to fashion in his hours of leisure ;
And, sitting rapt upon some wayside stone,
He wrought divinely with a knife alone.

He carved him castanets with fingers light,
So that his flock would follow him at night
Through the dark fields, obedient to their tones.
And on the ringing collars, and the bones
That served for bell-tongues, he would cut with skill
Faces and figures, flowers and birds, at will.

As for the goblet he was tendering,
You would have said that no such fairy thing
Was ever wrought by shepherd's knife or wit :
A full-flowered poppy wreathed the rim of it ;
And in among the languid flowers there
Two chamois browsed, and these the handles were.

A little lower down were maidens three,
And certes they were marvellous to see :
Near by, beneath a tree, a shepherd-lad
Slept, while on tiptoe stole the maidens glad,
And sought to seal his lips, ere he should waken,
With a grape-cluster from their basket taken.

Yet even now he smiles at their illusion,
So that the foremost maid is all confusion.
The odour of the goblet proved it new :
The giver had not drunk therefrom ; and you
Had said, but for their woody colouring,
The carven shapes were each a living thing.

Mirèio scanned the fair cup curiously.
"A tempting offering thine, shepherd!" said she:
But suddenly, "A finer one than this
Hath my heart's lord! Shepherd, his love it is!
Mine eyes close, his impassioned glances feeling:
I falter with the rapture o'er me stealing!"

So saying, she vanished like a tricksy sprite;
And Alari turned, and in the gray twilight
Ruefully, carefully, he folded up
And bore away again his carven cup,
Deeming it sad and strange this winsome elf
Her love should yield to any but himself.

Soon to the farm came suitor number two,
A keeper of wild horses from Sambu,—
Veran, by name. About his island bower
In the great prairies, where the asters flower,
He used to keep a hundred milk-white steeds,
Who nipped the heads of all the lofty reeds.

A hundred steeds! Their long manes flowing free
As the foam-crested billows of the sea!
Wavy and thick and all unshorn were they;
And when the horses on their headlong way
Plunged all together, their dishevelled hair
Seemed the white robes of creatures of the air.

I say it to the shame of human kind:
Camargan steeds were never known to mind
The cruel spur more than the coaxing hand.
Only a few or so, I understand,
By treachery seduced, have halter worn,
And from their own salt prairies been borne;

Yet the day comes when, with a vicious start,
Their riders throwing, suddenly they part,

And twenty leagues of land unresting scour,
Snuffing the wind, till Vacarès once more
They find, the salt air breathe, and joy to be
In freedom after ten years' slavery.

For these wild steeds are with the sea at home :
Have they not still the colour of the foam ?
Perchance they brake from old King Neptune's car ;
For when the sea turns dark and moans afar,
And the ships part their cables in the bay,
The stallions of Camargue rejoicing neigh,

Their sweeping tails like whipcord snapping loudly ;
Or pawing the earth, all, fiercely and proudly,
As though their flanks were stung as with a rod
By the sharp trident of the angry god,
Who makes the rain a deluge, and the ocean
Stirs to its depths in uttermost commotion.

And these were all Veran's.   Therefore one day
The island-chieftain paused upon his way
Across La Crau beside Mirèio's door ;
For she was famed, and shall be evermore,
For beauty, all about the delta wide
Where the great Rhone meeteth the ocean tide.

Confident came Veran to tell his passion,
With paletot, in the Arlesian fashion,
Long, light, and backward from his shoulders flowing ;
His gay-hued girdle like a lizard glowing,
The while his head an oil-skin cap protected,
Wherefrom the dazzling sun-rays were reflected.

And first the youth to Master Ramoun drew.
"Good-morrow to you, and good fortune too !"
He said.   "I come from the Camargan Rhone,
As keeper Pèire's grandson I am known.
Thou mindest him !   For twenty years or more
My grandsire's horses trod thy threshing-floor.

D

" Three dozen had the old man venerable,
As thou, beyond a doubt, rememberest well.
But would I, Master Ramoun, it were given
To thee to see the increase of that leaven !
Let ply the sickles ! We the rest will do,
For now have we an hundred lacking two ! "

" And long, my son," the old man said, " pray I
That you may see them feed and multiply.
I knew your grandsire well for no brief time ;
But now on him and me the hoary rime
Of age descends, and by the home lamp's ray
We sit content, and no more visits pay."

" But, Master Ramoun," cried the youthful lover,
" All that I want thou dost not yet discover !
For down at Sambu, in my island home,
When the Crau folk for loads of litter come,
And we help cord them down, it happens so
We talk sometimes about the girls of Crau.

" And thy Mirèio they have all portrayed
So charmingly, that, if thou wilt," he said,
" And if thou like me, I would gladly be
Thy son-in-law ! " " God grant me this to see ! "
Said Ramoun. " The brave scion of my friend
To me and mine can only honour lend."

Then did he fold his hands and them upraise
In saint-like gratitude. " And yet," he says,
" The child must like you too, O Veranet !
The only one will alway be a pet !
Meanwhile, in earnest of the dower I'll give her,
The blessing of the saints be yours for ever ! "

Forthwith summoned Ramoun his little daughter,
And told her of the friend who thus had sought her.

Pale, trembling, and afraid, " O father dear ! "
She said, " is not thy wisdom halting here ?
For I am but a child : thou dost forget.
Surely thou wouldst not send me from thee yet !

" Slowly, so thou hast often said to me,
Folk learn to love and live in harmony.
For one must know, and also must be known ;
And even then, my father, all's not done ! "
Here the dark shadow on her brow was lit
By some bright thought that e'en transfigured it.

So the drenched flowers, when morning rains are o'er,
Lift up their heavy heads, and smile once more.
Mirèio's mother held her daughter's view.
Then blandly rose the keeper, " Adieu,
Master," he said : " who in Camargue hath dwelt
Knows the mosquito-sting as soon as felt."

Also that summer came to Lotus Place
One from Petite Camargue, named Ourrias.
Breaker and brander of wild cattle, he ;
And black and furious all the cattle be
Over those briny pastures wild who run,
Maddened by flood and fog and scalding sun.

Alone this Ourrias had them all in charge
Summer and winter, where they roamed at large.
And so, among the cattle born and grown,
Their build, their cruel heart, became his own ;
His the wild eye, dark colour, dogged look.
How often, throwing off his coat, he took

His cudgel,—savage weaner !—never blenching,
And first the young calves from the udders wrenching,
Upon the wrathful mother fell so madly
That cudgel after cudgel brake he gladly,
Till she, by his brute fury masterèd,
Wild-eyed and lowing to the pine-copse fled !

Oft in the branding at Camargue had he
Oxen and heifers, two-year-olds and three,
Seized by the horns and stretched upon the ground.
His forehead bare the scar of an old wound
Fiery and forked like lightning.   It was said
That once the green plain with his blood was red.

On a great branding-day befell this thing :
To aid the mighty herd in mustering,
Li Santo, Agui Morto, Albaron,
And Faraman a hundred horsemen strong
Had sent into the desert.   And the herd
Roused from its briny lairs, and, forward spurred

By tridents of the branders close behind,
Fell on the land like a destroying wind.
Heifers and bulls in headlong gallop borne
Plunged, crushing centaury and salicorne ;
And at the branding-booth at last they mustered,
Just where a crowd three hundred strong had clustered.

A moment, as if scared, the beasts were still.
Then, when the cruel spur once more they feel,
They start afresh, into a run they break,
And thrice the circuit of the arena make ;
As marterns fly a dog, or hawks afar
By eagles in the Luberon hunted are.

Then Ourrias—what ne'er was done before—
Leaped from his horse beside the circus-door
Amid the crowd.   The cattle start again,
All saving five young bulls, and scour the plain ;
But these, with flaming eyes and horns defying
Heaven itself, are through the arena flying.

And he pursues them.   As a mighty wind
Drives on the clouds, he goads them from behind,

And presently outstrips them in the race ;
Then thumps them with the cruel goad he sways,
Dances before them as infuriate,
And lets them feel his own fists' heavy weight.

The people clap and shout, while Ourrias
White with Olympic dust encountered has
One bull, and seized him by the horns at length ;
And now 'tis head to muzzle, strength for strength.
The monster strans his prisoned horns to free
Until he bleeds, and bellows horribly.

But vain his fury, useless all his trouble !
The neatherd had the art to turn and double
And force the huge head with his shoulder round,
And shove it roughly back, till on the ground
Christian and beast together rolled, and made
A formless heap like some huge barricade.

The tamarisks are shaken by the cry
Of " Bravo Ourrias !   That's done valiantly ! "
While five stout youths the bull pin to the sward ;
And Ourrias, his triumph to record,
Seizes the red-hot iron with eager hand,
The vanquished monster on the hip to brand.

Then came a troop of girls on milk-white ponies,—
Arlesians,—flushed and panting every one is,
As o'er the arena at full gallop borne
They offer him a noble drinking-horn
Brimful of wine ; then turn and disappear,
Each followed by her faithful cavalier.

The hero heeds them not.   His mind is set
On the four monsters to be branded yet :
The mower toils the harder for the grass
He sees unmown.   And so this Ourrias
Fought the more savagely as his foes warmed,
And conquered in the end,—but not unharmed.

White-spotted and with horns magnificent,
The fourth beast grazed the green in all content.
"Now, man, enough !" in vain the neatherds shouted ;
Couched is the trident and the caution flouted ;
With perspiration streaming, bosom bare,
Ourrias the spotted bull charged then and there !

He meets his enemy, a blow delivers
Full in the face ; but ah ! the trident shivers.
The beast becomes a demon with the wound :
The brander grasps his horns, is whirled around,—
They start together, and are borne amain,
Crushing the salicornes along the plain.

The mounted herdsmen, on their long goads leaning,
Regard the mortal fray ; for each is meaning
Dire vengeance now.   The man the brute would crush,
The brute bears off the man with furious rush ;
The while with heavy, frothy tongue he clears
The blood that to his hanging lip adheres.

The brute prevailed.   The man fell dazed, and lay
Like a vile rakeful in the monster's way.
"Sham dead !" went up a cry of agony.
Vain words !   The beast his victim lifted high
On cruel horns and savage head inclined,
And flung him six and forty feet behind !

Once more a deafening outcry filled the place
And shook the tamarisks.   But Ourrias
Fell prone to earth, and ever after wore he
The ugly scar that marred his brow so sorely.
Now, mounted on his mare, he paces slow
With goad erect to seek Mirèio.

It chanced the little maid was all alone.
She had, that morning, to the fountain gone ;

And here, with sleeves and petticoats uprolled
And small feet dabbling in the water cold,
She was her cheese-forms cleaning with shave-grass;
And, lady saints! how beautiful she was!

"Good-morrow, pretty maid!" began the wooer,
" Thy forms will shine like mirrors, to be sure!
Will it offend thee, if I lead my mare
To drink out of thy limpid streamlet there?"
" Pray give her all thou wilt, at the dam head:
We've water here to spare!" the maiden said.

" Fair one!" spake the wild youth, "if e'er thou come
As pilgrim or as bride to make thy home
At Sylvarèal by the noisy wave, .
No life of toil like this down here thou'lt have!
Our fierce black cows are never milked, but these
Roam all at large, and women sit at ease."

"Young man, in cattle-land, I've heard them say,
Maids die of languor."—"Pretty maiden, nay:
There is no languor where two are together!"
" But brows are blistered in that burning weather,
And bitter waters drunk."—"When the sun shines,
My lady, thou shalt sit beneath the pines!"

" Ah! but they say, young man, those pines are laden
With coils of emerald serpents."—"Fairest maiden,
We've herons also, and flamingoes red
That chase them down the Rhone with wings outspread
Like rosy scarfs."—"Then, I would have thee know
Lotus and pine too far asunder grow!"

" But priests and maids, my beauty, ne'er can tell,
The saw affirms, the land where they may dwell
And eat their bread."—" Let mine but eaten be
With him I love: that were enough," said she,
" To lure me from the home-nest to remove."
" If that be so, sweet one, give me thy love!"

"Thy suit," Mirèio said, "mayhap I'll grant!
But first, young man, yon water-lily plant
Will bear a cluster of columbine grapes.
Yon hills will melt from all their solid shapes,
That goad will flower, and all the world will go
In boats unto the citadel of Baux!"

CANTO V.

The Battle.

COOL with the coming eve the wind was blowing,
  The shadows of the poplars longer growing ;
Yet still the westering sun was two hours high,
As the tired ploughman noted wistfully,—
Two hours of toil ere the fresh twilight come,
And wifely greeting by the door at home.

But Ourrias the brander left the spring,
The insult he had suffered pondering.
So moved to wrath was he, so stung with shame,
The blood into his very forehead came ;
And, muttering deadly spite beneath his teeth,
He drave at headlong gallop o'er the heath.

As damsons in a bush, the stones of Crau
Are plentiful ; and Ourrias, fuming so,
Would gladly with the senseless flints have striven,
Or through the sun itself his lance have driven.
A wild boar from its lair forced to decamp,
And scour the desert slopes of black Oulympe.

Ere turning on the dogs upon his track,
Erects the rugged bristles of his back,
And whets his tusks upon the mountain oaks.
And now young Vincen with his comely looks
Must needs have chosen the herdsman's very path,
And meets him squarely, boiling o'er with wrath.

D*

Whereas the simple dreamer wandered smiling,
His memory with a sweet tale beguiling,
That he had heard a fond girl whispering
Beneath a mulberry-tree one morn in spring.
Straight is he as a cane from the Durance ;
And love, peace, joy, beam from his countenance.

The soft air swells his loose, unbottoned shirt :
His firm, bare feet are by the stones unhurt,
And light as lizard slips he o'er the way.
Oh ! many a time, when eve was cool and gray,
And all the land in shadow lay concealed,
He used to roam about the darkling field,

Where the chill airs had shut the tender clover ;
Or, like a butterfly, descend and hover
Around the homestead of Mirèio ;
Or, hidden cleverly, his hiding show,
Like a gold-crested or an ivy wren,
By a soft chirrup uttered now and then.

And she would know who called her, and would fly
Swift, silent, to the mulberry-tree hard by,
With quickened pulses.   Fair is the moonlight
Upon narcissus-buds in summer night,
And sweet the rustle of the zephyr borne
In summer eve over the ripening corn,

Until the whole, in infinite undulation,
Seems like a great heart palpitant with passion.
Also the chamois hath a joy most keen
When through the Queiras, that most wild ravine
All day before the huntsman he hath flown,
And stands at length upon a peak, alone

With larches and with ice fields, looking forth.
But all these joys and charms are little worth,

With the brief rapture of the hours compared—
Ah, brief!—that Vincen and Mirèio shared,
When, by the friendly shadows favourèd,
(Speak low, my lips, for trees can hear, 'tis said,)

Their hands would seek each other and would meet,
And silence fall upon them, while their feet
Played idly with the pebbles in their way.
Until, not knowing better what to say,
The tyro-lover laughingly would tell
Of all the small mishaps that him befell;

Of nights he passed beneath the open heaven;
Of bites the farmers' dogs his legs had given,
And show his scars.   And then the maid told o'er
Her tasks of that day and the day before;
And what her parents said; and how the goat
With trellis-flowers had filled his greedy throat.

Once only—Vincen knew not what he did;
But, stealthy as a wild-cat, he had slid
Along the grasses of the barren moor,
And prostrate lay his darling's feet before.
Then—soft, my lips, because the trees can hear—
He said, " Give me one kiss, Mirèio dear!

"I cannot eat nor drink," he made his moan,
"For the great love I bear you!   Yea, mine own,
Your breath the life out of my blood has taken.
Go not, Mirèio!   Leave me not forsaken!
From dawn to dawn, at least, let a true lover
Kneel, and your garment's hem with kisses cover! '

" Why, Vincen," said Mirèio, " that were sin!
Then would the black-cap and the penduline
Tell everywhere the secret they had heard!"
" No fear of that! for every tell-tale bird
I'd banish from La Crau to Arles," said he;
" For you, Mirèio, are as heaven to me!

" Now list !   There grows a plant in river Rhone,
Eel-grass, the name whereby that plant is known,
Two flowers it beareth, each on its own stem,
And a great space of water severs them,
For the plant springs out of the river's bed ;
But when the time for wooing comes," he said,

" One flower leaps to the surface of the flood,
And in the genial sunshine opes its bud.
Whereon the other, seeing this so fair,
Swims eagerly to seize and kiss her there ;
But, for the tangled weeds, can she not gain
Her love, till her frail stem breaks with the strain.

" Now free at last, but dying, she doth raise
Her pale lips for her sister's last embrace.
So I !   One kiss, and I will die to-night !
We are all alone ! "   Mirèio's cheek grew white.
Then sprang he, wild-eyed as a lissome beast,
And clasped her.   Hurriedly the maid released

Herself from his too daring touch.   Once more
He strove to seize,—but ah ! my lips, speak lower,
For the trees hear,—" Give over ! " cried the girl,
And all her slender frame did writhe and curl.
Yet would he frantic cling ; but straight thereafter
She pinched him, bent, slipped, and, with ringing laughter,

The saucy little damsel sped away,
And lifted up her voice in mocking lay.
So did these two, upon the twilight wold
Their moon-wheat sow, after the proverb old.
Flowery the moments were, and fleet with pleasure :
Of such our Lord giveth abundant measure

To peasants and to kings alike.   And so
I come to what befell that eve on Crau.

Ourrias and Vincen met.   As lightning cleaves
The first tall tree, Ourrias his wrath relieves.
" 'Tis you son of a hag, for aught I know,
Who have bewitched her,—this Mirèio ;

" And since your path would seem to lie her way,
Tell her, tatterdemalion, what I say !
No more for her nor for her weasel face
Care I than for the ancient clout," he says,
" That from your shoulders fluttering I see.
Go, pretty coxcomb, tell her this from me !"

Stopped Vincen thunderstruck.   His wrath leaped high
As leaps a fiery rocket to the sky.
" Is it your pleasure that I strangle you,
Base churl,' he said, "or double you in two ?"
And faced him with a look he well might dread,
As when a starving leopard turns her head.

His face was purple, quivered all his frame.
" Oh, better try !" the mocking answer came.
" You'll roll headfirst upon the gravel, neighbour !
Bah, puny hands ! meet for no better labour
Than to twist osiers when they're supple made ;
Or to rob hen-roosts, lurking in the shade !"

Stung by the insult, " Yea, I can twist osier,
And I can twist your neck with all composure,"
Said Vincen.   " Coward, it were well you ran !
Else vow I by St. James the Gallican,
You'll never see your tamarisks any more !
This iron first shall bray your limbs before !"

Wondering, and charmed to find by such quick chance
A man whereon to wreak his vengeance,
" Wait !" said the herdsman : "be not over-hot !
First let me have a pipe, young idiot !"
And brought to light a buckskin pouch, and set
Between his teeth a broken calumet.

Then scornfully, "While rocking you, my lamb,
Under the goose-foot, did your gypsy-dam
Ne'er tell the tale of Jan de l'Ours, I pray?—
Two men in one, who, having gone one day,
By orders, to plough stubble with two yoke,
Seized plough and teams, as shepherds do a crook,

"And hurled them o'er a poplar-tree hard by?
Well for you, urchin, there's no poplar nigh!
You couldn't lead a stray ass whence it came!"
But Vincen stood like pointer to the game.
"I say," he roared in tones stentorian,
"Will you come down, or must I fetch you, man

"Or hog? Come! Brag no more your beast astride
You flinch now we are going to decide
Which sucked the better milk, or you or I?
Was it you, bearded scoundrel? We will try!
Why, I will tread you like a sheaf of wheat,
If you dare flout yon maiden true and sweet.

"No fairer flower in this land blossomed ever;
And I who am called Vincen, basket-weaver,
Yes, I—her suitor, be it understood—
Will wash your slanders out in your own blood,
If such you have!" Quoth Qurrias, "I am ready,
My gypsy-suitor to a cupboard! Steady!"

Therewith alights. They fling their coats away,
Fists fly, and pebbles roll before the fray.
They fall upon each other in the manner
Of two young bulls who, in the vast savannah,
Where the great sun glares in the tropic sky,
The sleek sides of a dark young heifer spy

In the tall grasses, lowing amorous.
The thunder bursts within them, challenged thus.

Mad, blind with love, they paw, they stare, they spring ;
And furious charge, their muzzles lowering ;
Retire, and charge again.   The ominous sound
Of crashing horns fills all the spaces round.

And long, I ween, the battle is, and dire.
The combatants are maddened by desire.
Puissant Love urges and goads them on.
So here, with either doughty champion.
'Twas Ourrias who received the first hard touch ;
And, being threatened with another such,

Lifts his huge fist and lays young Vincen flat
As with a club.   "There, urchin, parry that !"
"See if I have a scratch, man !" cried the lad.
The other, "Bastard, count the knocks you've had !"
"Count you the ounces of hot blood," he shouted,
"Monster, that from your flattened nose have spouted !"

And then they grapple ; bend and stretch their best,
With foot to foot, shoulder to shoulder, prest.
Their arms are wreathed and coiled like serpents fell
The veins within their necks to bursting swell
And tense their muscles with the mighty strain.
Long time they stiff and motionless remain,

With pulsing flanks, like flap of bustard's wing.
And, one against the other steadying,
Bear up like the abutments huge and wide
Of that great bridge the Gardoun doth bestride.
Anon they part : their doubled fists upraise,
Once more the pestle in the mortar brays,

And in their fury ply they tooth or nail.
Good God ! the blows of Vincen fall like hail.
Yet ah ! what club-like hits the herdsman deals !
And, as their crushing weight the weaver feels,
He whirls as whirls a sling about his foe,
And backward bends to deal his fiercest blow.

"Look your last, villain !" Ere the word said he,
The mighty herdsman seized him bodily,
And flung him o'er his shoulder far away,
As a Provençal shovels wheat.   He lay
A moment on his side, not sorely hurt.
"Pick up, O worm !" cried Ourrias,—"pick the dirt

"You have displaced, and eat it, if you will !"
"Enough of that !   Brute who was broken ill,
We'll have three rounds before this game is over !"
With bitter hate retorts the poor boy-lover ;
And, reddening to his very hair for shame,
Rears like a dragon to retrieve his fame.

And, daring death, he on the brute hath flown,
And dealt a blow marvellous in such an one
Straight from the shoulder to the other's breast,
Who reeled and groped for that whereon to rest,
With darkening eyes and brow cold-beaded, till
He crashed to earth, and all La Crau was still.

Its misty limit blent with the far sea ;
The sea's with the blue ether, dreamily.
Still in mid-air there floated shining things,
Swans, and flamingoes on their rosy wings,
Come to salute the last of the sunset
Along the desert meres that glimmered yet.

The white mare of the herdsman lazily
Pulled at the dwarf-oak leaves that grew thereby :
The iron stirrups of the creature jangled,
As loose and heavy at her sides they dangled.
"Stir, and I crush you, ruffian !" Vincen said :
"'Tis not by feet that men are measurèd !"

Then in the silent wold the victor pressed
His heel upon the brander's prostrate breast,

Who writhed beneath it vainly, while the blood
Sluggish and dark from lips and nostrils flowed.
Thrice did he strive the horny foot to move,
And thrice the basket-weaver from above

Dealt him a blow that levelled him once more,
Until he haggard lay, and gasping sore
Like some sea-monster. "So your mother, then,
Was not, it seems, the only mould of men,"
Said Vincen, jeeringly. "Go tell the tale
Of my fist's weight to bulls in Sylvarèal.

"Go to the waste of the Camargan isle,
And hide your bruises and your shame awhile
Among your beasts!" So saying, he loosed his hold,
As some great ram, a shearer in the fold
Pins with his knees till shorn; then, with a blow
Upon the crupper, bids him freely go.

Bursting with rage and all defiled with dust,
The herdsman went his ways. But wherefore must
He linger ferreting about the heath,
Amid the oaks and broom, under his breath
Muttering curses? until suddenly
He stoops, then swings his savage trident high,

And darts on Vincen. For him all is done.
Vain were the hope that murderous lance to shun,
And the boy paled as on the day he died;
Not fearing death, but that he could not bide
The treachery. A felon's prey to be!
That stung the manly soul to agony.

"Traitor, you dare not!" But the lad restrains
The word, firm as a martyr in his pains;
For yon's the farmstead hidden by the trees.
Tenderly, wistfully, he turns to these.
"O my Mirèio!" said the eager eye,
"Look hither, darling,—'tis for you I die!"

Great heart, intent as ever on his love!
" Say your prayers ! " thundered Ourrias from above
In a hoarse voice, and pitiless to hear,
And pierced the victim with his iron spear.
Then, with a heavy groan, the fated lover
Upon the green-sward rolled, and all was over.

The beaten grass is dark with human gore,
And the field-ants already coursing o'er
The prostrate limbs ere Ourrias mounts, and hies
Under the rising moon in frantic wise ;
Muttering, as the flints beneath him fly,
" To-night the Crau wolves will feast merrily."

Deep stillness reigned in Crau.   Its limit dim
Blent with the sea's on the horizon's rim,
The sea's with the blue ether.   Gleaming things,
Swans, and flamingoes on their ruddy wings,
Came to salute the last declining light
Among the desert meres that glimmered white.

Away, Ourrias, away !   Draw not the rein,
Urge thy unresting gallop o'er the plain,
While the green heron shout their fearsome cries
In thy mare's ear, as the good creature flies,
Till her ear trembles, and her nostrils quiver,
And eyes dilate.   That night the great Rhone River

Slept on his stony bed beneath the moon,
As pilgrim of Sainte Baume may lay him down,
Fevered and weary, in a deep ravine.
" Ho ! " cries the ruffian to three boatmen seen,
" Ho ! Boat ahoy ! We must cross, hark ye there !
On board or in the hold, I and my mare ! "

" On board, my hearty, then, without delay !
There shines the night-lamp ! And lured by its ray,"

Answered a cheery voice, "about our prow
And oars the fish frisk playfully enow.
It is good fishing, and the hour is fair.
On board at once! We have no time to spare."

Therewith upon the poop the villain clomb.
While, tethered to the stern, amid the foam
Swam the white mare. Now fishes huge and scaly
Forsook their grottoes, and leaped upward gayly,
And flashed on the smooth surface of the stream.
"Have a care, pilot! For this craft I deem

" Nowise too sound." And he who spake once more
Lay foot to stretcher, bent the supple oar.
" So I perceive. Ah!" was the pilot's word,
" I tell thee we've an evil freight on board."
No more. And all the while the vessel old
Staggered and pitched and like a drunkard rolled.

A crazy craft! Rotten its timbers all.
" Thunder of God!" Ourrias began to call,
Seizing the helm his tottering feet to stay.
Whereon the boat in some mysterious way
Seemed moved to writhing, as a wounded snake
Whose back a shepherd with a stone doth break.

" Doth all this tumult, comrades, bode disaster?"
Appealed the brander, growing pale as plaster.
" And will you drown me?" Brake the pilot out,
" I cannot hold the craft! She springs about
And wriggles like a carp. Villain, I know
You've murdered some one, and not long ago!"

" Who told you that? May Satan if I have
Thrust me with his pitch-fork beneath the wave."
" Ah!" said the livid pilot, "then I err!
I had forgot the cause of all this stir.
'Tis Saint Medard's to-night, when poor drowned men
Come from their dismal pits to land again,

" How deep and dark soe'er their watery prison.
Look !   Even now hath from the wave arisen
The long procession of the weeping dead !
Barefoot, poor things! the shingly shore they tread,
The turbid water dripping, dripping, see,
From matted hair and stained clothes heavily.

" See them defile under the poplars tall,
Carrying lighted tapers, one and all.
While up the river's bank, now and anon,
Eagerly clambereth another one.
'Tis they who toss our wretched craft about
So like a raging storm, I make no doubt.

" Their cramped legs and their mottled arms—ah, see !—
And heavy heads they from the weeds would free.
Oh, how they watch the stars as on they go,
Quaff the fresh air and thrill at sight of Crau,
And scent the harvest odours the winds bring,
In their brief hour of motion revelling !

" And still the water from their garments raineth,
And still another and another gaineth
The river-bank.   And there," the boatman moans,
" Are the old men, women, and little ones :
They spurn the clinging mud.   Ah me !" he said,
" Yon ghastly things abhor the fisher's trade.

" The lamprey and the perch they made their game,
And now are they become food for the same.
But what is this?   Another piteous band,
Travelling in a line along the sand ?
Ah, yes ! the poor deserted maids," quoth he,
" Who asked the Rhone for hospitality,

" And sought to hide their shame in the great river.
Alas ! alas !   They seem to moan for ever.

And, oh, how painfully, fond hearts, ill fated,
Labour the bosoms by the dank weeds weighted !
Is it the water dripping that one hears
From their long veils of hair, or is it tears?"

He ceased.   The wending souls bare each a light,
Intently following in the silent night
The river-shore.   And those two listening
Might even have heard the whirr of a moth's wing.
"Are they not, pilot," asked the awe-struck brander,
" Seeking somewhat in the gloom where they wander?"

"Ah, yes, poor things ! " the master-boatman said.
"See how from side to side is turned each head.
'Tis their good works they seek,—their acts of faith
Sown upon earth ere their untimely death.
And when they spy the same, 'tis said moreover,
They haste thereto, as haste the sheep to clover,

"The good work or the act of faith to cull.
And when of such as these their hands are full,
Lo, they all turn to flowers !   And they who gather
Go tender them with joy to God the Father,
Being by the flowers to Peter's gate conveyed.
Thus those who find a watery grave," he said,

"The gracious God granteth a respite to,
That they may save themselves.   But some anew
Ere the day dawn will bury their good deeds
Deep underneath the surging river-weeds.
And some," the pilot whispered,—"some are worse,
Devourers of the needy, *murderers*,

" Atheists, traitors, that worm-eaten kind.
These hunt the river-shore, but only find
Their sins and crimes like great stones in the gravel
Whereon their bare feet stumble as they travel.
The mule when dead is beaten never more ;
But these God's mercy shall in vain implore

" Under the roaring wave." Here, sore afraid,
Ourrias a hand upon the pilot laid,
Like robber at a turning. "Look!" he cries,
" There's water in the hold!" Whereon replies
The pilot, coolly, " And the bucket's there!"
The herdsman bales for life in his despair.

Ay, bale, brave Ourrias! But there danced that night,
On Trincataio bridge, the water-sprite.
Madly the white mare strove to break her halter.
" What ails you, Blanco?" Ourrias 'gan falter.
" Fear you the dead yonder upon the verge?"
Over the gunnel plashed the rising surge.

"Captain, the craft sinks, and I cannot swim!"
" I know no help," the pilot answered him.
" We must go down. But, presently," he said,
" A cable will be heaved us by the dead,—
The dead you fear so,—on the river-bank."
And even as he spake the vessel sank.

The tapers gleaming far and fitfully
In the poor ghostly hands flared forth so high,
They sent a shaft of vivid brilliance
Across the murky river's broad expanse;
Then, as a spider in the morn you see
Glide o'er his late-spun thread, the boatmen three,

Being all spirits, leaped out of the stream,
And caught and swooped along the dazzling beam.
And Ourrias, too, the cable sought to seize
Amid the gurgling waters, even as these;
But sought it vainly. And the water-sprite
Danced upon Trincataio bridge that night.

CANTO VI.

The Witch.

THE merry birds, until the white dawn showeth
   Clear in the east, are silent every one.
Silent the odorous Earth until she knoweth
In her warm heart the coming of the Sun,
As maiden in her fairest robes bedight
Breathless awaits her lover and her flight.

Across La Crau three swineherds held their way
From St. Chamas the wealthy, whither they
Had to the market gone.   Their herds were sold,
And o'er their shoulders pouches full of gold
Were hung, and by their hanging cloaks concealed :
So, chatting idly, they attained the field

Of the late strife.   Suddenly one cried, " Hush !
Comrades, I hear a moaning in the bush."
" 'Tis but a tolling bell," the rest averred,
" From Saint Martin's or from Maussano heard,
Or the north wind the dwarf-oak limbs a-swaying."
But, ere they spake, all were their steps delaying,

Arrested by so piteous a groan
It rent the very heart.   And every one
Cried, " Holy Jesus !   Here has been foul play ! "
Then crossed themselves, and gently took their way
Toward the sound.   Ah, what a sight there was !
Vincen, supine upon the stony grass,—

The grass blood-stained, the trampled earth besprent
With willow rods.   IIis shirt to ribbons rent,
Stabbed in the breast, left on the moor alone,
Had lain the poor lad through the night now gone,
With but the stars to watch.   But the dim ray
Of early dawn, as ebbed his life away,

Falling upon his lids had oped them wide.
Straightway the good Samaritans turned aside
From their home-path, stooped, and a hammock made
Of their three cloaks, thereon the victim laid,
Then bare him tenderly upon their arms
Unto the nearest door,—the Lotus-Farm's. . . .

O friends,—Provençal poets brave and dear,
Who love my songs of other days to hear !
You, Roumanille, who blend with songs you sing
Tears, girlish laughter, and the breath of spring ;
And you, proud Aubanel, who stray where quiver
The changing lights and shades of wood and river,

To soothe a heart oppressed by love's fond dream ;
You, Crousillat, who your belovèd stream,
The bright Touloubro, make more truly famous
Than did the grim star-gazer Nostradamus ;
And you, Anselme, who see, half-sad, half-smiling,
Fair girls under the trellised arbours whiling

Their hours away ; and you, my Paul, the witty,
And peasant Tavan, who attune your ditty
Unto the crickets' chirrup, while you peer
Wistful at your poor pickaxe ; and most dear,
Adolphe Dumas, who when Durance is deep
With his spring flood, come back your thoughts to steep,

And warm the Frenchman at Provençal suns,
'Twas you who met my own Mirèio once

At your great Paris,—met her tenderly,
Where she had flown, impetuous, daring, shy;
And last Garcin, brave son of a brave sire,
Whose soul mounts upward on a wind of fire ;—

Upbear me with your holy breath as now
I climb for the fair fruit on that high bough ! . . .
The swineherds paused at Master Ramoun's door,
Crying, "Good-morrow !   Yonder, on the moor,
We found this poor lad wounded in the breast.
'Twere well that his sore hurt were quickly drest."

So laid their burden on the broad, flat stone.
They tell Mirèio, to the garden gone
To gather fruit, who, basket on her side,
Fled wildly to the spot.   Thither, too, hied
The labourers all ; but she, her basket falling,
Stretched forth her hands on Mother Mary calling.

"Vincen is bleeding!   Ah, what have they done?"
Then, lovingly, the head of the dear one
She lifted, turned, and long and mutely gazed
As though with horror and with grief amazed,
Her large tears dropping fast.   And well he knows
That tender touch to be Mirèio's,

And faintly breathes, " Pity, and pray for me,
Because I need the good God's company ! "
" Your parched throat moisten with this cordial.   Strive
To drink," old Ramoun said : "you will revive."
The maiden seized the cup, and drop by drop
She made him drink, and spake to him of hope

Till his pain lulled.   " May God keep you alway
From such distress, and your sweet care repay ! "
Said Vincen ; and the brave boy would not tell
It was for her sake that he fought and fell ;
But " Splitting osier on my breast," he said,
" The sharp knife slipped, and pierced me."   Therewith
          strayed

E

His thought back to his love as bee to flower.
" The anguish on thy face, dear, in this hour
Is far more bitter than my wound to me.
The pretty basket that in company
We once began will be unfinished now.
Would I had seen it full to overflow,

" Dear, with thy love ! Oh, stay ! Life's in thine eyes.
Ah, if thou couldst do something," the lad cries,
" For him,—the poor old basket-weaver there,—
My father, worn with toil ! " In her despair,
Mirèio bathes the wound, while some bring lint,
And some run to the hills for healing mint.

Then the maid's mother spake : " Let four men rally,
And to the Fairies' Cavern, in the valley
They call Enfer, bear up this wounded man.
The deadlier the hurt, the sooner can
The old witch heal. Scale first the cliffs of Baux,
And circling vultures the cave's mouth will show."

A hole flush with the rocks, by lizards haunted,
And veiled by tufts of rosemary thereby planted.
For ever, since the holy Angelus swells,
In Mary's honour from the minster-bells,
The antique fairies have been forced to hide
From sunlight, and in this deep cavern bide.

Strange, airy things, they used to flit about
Dimly, 'twixt form and substance, in and out :
Half-earthly made, to be the visible
Spirit of Nature ; female made as well,
To tame the savagery of primal men.
But these were fair in fairies' eyes, and then

They loved : and so, infatuate, lifted not
Mortals unto their own celestial lot ;

But, lusting, fell into our low estate,
As birds fall, whom a snake doth fascinate,
From their high places. But, while thus I write,
The bearers have borne Vincen up the height.

A dim, straight passage led the cavern toward,
A rocky funnel where they gently lowered
The sufferer ; and he did not go alone,—
Yet was Mirèio's self the only one
Who dared to follow down that awesome road,
Commending, as she went, his soul to God.

The bottom gained, they found a grotto cold
And vast ; midway whereof a beldam old,
The witch Taven, sat silent, crouching lowly
As lost in thought and utter melancholy,
Holding a sprig of brome, and muttering,
" Some call thee devil's wheat, poor little thing,

" Yet art thou one of God's own signs for good ! "
Therewith Mirèio, trembling where she stood,
Was fain to tell why they had sought her thus.
" I knew it ! " cried the witch, impervious,
The brome addressing still, with bended head.
" Thou poor field-flower !   The trampling flock," she
        said,

" Browse on thy leaves and stems the whole year long ;
But all the more thou spreadest and art strong,
And north and south with verdure deckest yet."
She ceased.   A dim light, in a snail-shell set,
Danced o'er the dank rock-wall in lurid search :
Here hung a sieve ; there, on a forkèd perch,

Roosted a raven, a white hen beside.
Suddenly, as if drunken, rose and cried
The witch, " And what care I whoe'er you be ?
Faith walketh blindfold, so doth Charity,
Nor from her even tenor wandereth.
Say, Valabregan weaver, have you faith ? "

"I have." Then wildly, their pursuit inviting,
Like a she-wolf her flanks with her tail smiting,
Darted the hag into a deeper shaft,
While the fowl cackled and the raven laughed
Before her footsteps; and the boy and maid
Followed her through the darkness, sore afraid.

"Stay not!" she cried. "The time is now to find
The mystic mandrake." And, with hands entwined,
Obedient to the voice the two crept on,
Through the infernal passage, till they won
A grotto larger than the rest. "Lo! now,
Lord Nostradamus' plant, the golden bough,

"The staff of Joseph and the rod of Moses!"
Thus crying, Taven a slender shrub discloses,
And, kneeling, with her chaplet crowns. Then said,
Arising, "We too must be garlanded
With mandrake;" and the plant in the rock's cleft
Of three fair sprays mysteriously bereft,

Herself crowned first, and next the wounded man,
And last the maid. Then, crying, "Forward!" ran
Down the weird way, before her footsteps lit
By shining beetles trooping over it.
Yet turned with a sage word,—"All paths of glory,
My children, have their space of purgatory!

"Therefore have courage! for we must, alas!
The terrors of the Sabatori pass."
And, while she spake, their faces cut they find,
And breathing stopped, by rush of keenest wind.
"Lie down!" she whispered hurriedly,—"lie low!
The triumph of the Whirlwind Sprites is now!"

Then fell upon them, like a sudden gale
Or white squall on the water fraught with hail,

A swarm of whirling, yelping, vicious things,
Under the fanning of whose icy wings
The mortals, drenched with sweat and struck with cold,
Stood shivering.   " Away, ye over-bold,

" Ye spoilers of the harvest, unlicked whelps ! "
Taven exclaimed.   " Must we then use such helps
To the fair deeds we do ?   Yet, as by skill
The sage physician bringeth good from ill,
We witches, by our hidden arts, compel
Evil to yield its fruit of good as well.

" Naught's hid from us.   For where the vulgar see
A stone, a whip, a stag, a malady,
We witches can the inner force divine
Like that which works under the scum of wine
In fermentation.   Pierce the vat, you know,
A seething, boiling scum will outward flow.

" Find, if you can, the key of Solomon !
Or speak unto the mountain in its own
Dread language !   It shall move at your behest,
And roll into the valley ere it rest."
Meanwhile they wended lower, and were 'ware
Of a small, roguish voice a-piping there,

Most like a goldfinch : " Our good granny spins,
And winds and spins, and then anew begins,
And thinks that she spins worsted night and day,
And ha ! ha ! gossip, she spins only hay !
Te ! he ! spin, Aunty, spin ! " And long-drawn laughter,
Like whinnying of young colts, followed thereafter.

" Why, what can that be ? " asked Mirèio,—
" The little voice that laughs and jeers us so ?"
Again the childish treble came, " Te ! he !
Who is this pretty mortal ?   Let us see !
We'll raise the neckerchief a little bit :
Are nuts and pomegranates under it ?"

Then the poor maid had nearly cried outright ;
But the hag stayed her, " Here's no cause for fright.
The singing, jeering thing is but a Glari :
Fantasti is his name, a sprightly fairy.
In his good mood he will your kitchen sweep,
Mind fire, turn roast, and a full hen's-nest keep.

" But what a marplot when he takes the whim !
He'll salt your broth just as it pleaseth him,
Or blow your light out ere you're half in bed !
Or, if to vespers you would go," she said,
" At Saint Trophime, in all your best bedight,
He'll hide your Sunday suit, or spoil it quite ! "

" Hear !" shrieked the imp : "now hear the old hag
    talk !
'Tis like the creak of an ill-greasèd block !
No doubt, my withered olive," the thing said,
" I twitch the bedclothes off a sleeping maid
Sometimes at midnight, and she starts with fear
And trembles, and her breast heaves.   Oh, I see her !"

And with its whinnying laugh the sprite was gone ;
Then, for a brief space, as they journeyed on
Under the grots, the witcheries were stayed ;
And in the gloomy silence, long delayed,
They heard the water drop from vaulted roof
To crystal ground.   Now there had sat aloof,

Upon a ledge of rock, a tall, white thing,
Which rose in the half-light as menacing
With one long arm.   Then stiff as a quartz rock
Stood Vincen ; while, transported by the shock,
Mirèio would have leaped a precipice,
Had such been there.   " Old scare-crow, what is this?

" What mean you," cried Taven, " by swaying so
Your limp head like a poplar to and fro ?"

Then turning to the stricken twain, " My dears,
You know the Laundress? Oft-times she appears
On Mount Ventour, and then the common crowd
Are wont to take her for a long, white cloud.

" But shepherds, when they see her, pen their sheep.
The Laundress of destruction, who doth keep
The errant clouds in hand, is known too well.
She scrubs them with a strength right terrible ;
Wringing out buckets full of rain, and flame.
And neatherds house their cattle at her name ;

" And seamen, on the angry, tossing wave,
Upon our Lady call, their craft to save."
Here drowned her speech a discord most appalling,
Rattling of latches, whimpering, caterwauling,
With uncouth words half-uttered intervening,
Whereof the devil only knows the meaning ;

And brazen din through all the cave resounding,
As one were on a witch-caldron pounding.
Then whence those shrieks of laughter, and those wails
As of a woman in her pains ? Prevails
Hardly amid the howl the beldam's speech,
" Give me a hand that I may hold you each,

" And let your magic garlands not be lost ! "
Here were they jostled from their feet almost
By rush of something puffing, grunting, snorting,
Most like a herd of ghostly swine comporting.
On starlit winter-nights, when Nature slumbers
Under her snowy sheets, come forth in numbers

The fowlers, torch in hand, who bush and tree
By river-side will beat right vigorously,
Till all the birds at roost arise in haste,
And, as by breath of smithy-bellows chased,
Affrighted, rush until the net receive :
So drave Taven the foul herd with her sieve

Into the outer darkness.　With the same
She circles traced, luminous, red as flame,
And divers other figures.　All the while,
" Avaunt ! " she cried, " ye locusts, ye who spoil
The harvest !　Quit my sight, or woe betide you !
Workers of evil, in your burrows hide you !

" Since, by the pricking of your flesh, ye know
The hills are still with sunshine all aglow,
Go hang yourselves again on the rock-angles,
Ye bats ! " They flit.　The clamour disentangles,
And dies away.　Then to the children spake
The witch : " All birds of night themselves betake

" To this retreat what time shines the daylight
On the ploughed land and fallow ; but at night,—
At night the lamps are lighted without hand
In churches void and triply fastened, and
The bells toll of themselves, and pavement stones
Upstart, and tremble all the buried bones,

" And the poor dead arise and kneel to pray,
And mass is said by priests as pale as they.
Ask the owls else, who clamber down the steeple
To drain the lamps of oil ; and if the people
Who thus partake of the communion
Be not all dead except the priests alone !

" What time the beldam jeers at February,
Let women everywhere be wondrous wary,
Nor fall asleep on chairs for awful reason !
Shepherds as well, at yon uncanny season
Early your charges fold, and it mislike you
A spell should motionless and rigid strike you

' For seven years' time.　The Fairies' Cavern, too,
Looses about these days its eerie crew.

Winged or four-footed, they o'er Crau disperse ;
While, from their lairs aroused, the sorcerers
Gather, the *farandoulo* dance, and sup
An evil potion from a golden cup.

" The dwarf-oaks dance as well. Lord, how they trip it !
Meanwhile there's Garamaude in wait for Gripet.
Fie, cruel flirt ! Ay, seize the carrion,
And claw her bowels out ! Now they are gone,—
Nay, but they come again ! And, oh, despair !
The monster stealing through the sea-kale there,

" The one who like a burglar crouched and ran,
Is Bambarouche, babe-stealing harridan.
Her wailing prey in her long claw she takes,
Lifts on her horny head, and off she makes.
And yon's another ! She's the Nightmare-sprite
Comes down the chimney-flue at dead of night,

" And stealthy climbs upon the sleeper's breast,
Who, as with weight of a tall tower opprest,
Hath horrid dreams. Hi ! What a hideous racket !
My dears, 'tis the foul-weather fiends who make it !
That sound of rusty hinges, groaning doors,
Is they who beat up fog upon the moors,

" And ride the winds that homestead-roofs uptear
And bear afar. Ha, Moon ! What ails you there ?
What dire indignity hath made you scowl
So red and large o'er Baux ? 'Ware the dog's howl !
Yon dog can snap you like a cake, be sure !
He minds the filthy Demon of the Sewer !

" Now see the holm-oaks bend their heads like ferns,
And see that flame that leaps and writhes and burns.
It is St. Elmo's. And that ringing sound
Of rapid hoofs upon the stony ground
Is the wild huntsman riding over Crau."
Here hoarse and breathless paused the witch of Baux.

E*

But straight thereafter, "Cover ears and eyes,
For the black lamb is bleating!" wildly cries.
"That baaing lambkin!" Vincen dared to say;
But she, "Hide eyes and ears without delay!
Woe to the stumbler here! Sambuco's Path
Less peril than the black horn's passage hath.

"Tender his bleating, as you hear, and soft:
Thereby he lures to their destruction oft
The heedless Christians who attend his moan.
To them he shows the sheen of Herod's throne,
The gold of Judas, and the fatal spot
Where Saracens made fast the golden goat.

"Her they may milk till death, to hearts' content.
But, when they call for their last sacrament,
The black lamb only buts them savagely.
And yet, so evil is the time," quoth she,
"Unnumbered greedy souls that bait will seize,
Burn incense unto gold, then die as these!"

Now, while the white hen gave three piercing crows,
The eerie guide did to her guests disclose
The thirteenth grotto, and the last; and lo!
A huge, wide chimney and a hearth aglow,
And seven black tom-cats warming round the flame;
And, hanging from a 'hook above the same,

An iron caldron of gigantic size,
And underneath two fire-brands, dragon-wise
Belching blue flame. "Is.it with these you brew,
Grandmother," asked the lad, "your magic stew?"
"With these, my son. They're branches of wild vine:
No better logs for burning be than mine."

"Well, call them branches if it be your taste;
But—but I may not jest. Haste, mother, haste!"

Now, midway of the grotto, they descry
A large, round table of red porphyry ;
And, radiating from this wondrous place,
Lower than root of oak or mountain base,

Infinite aisles whose gleaming columns cluster
Like pendant icicles in shape and lustre.
These are the far-famed galleries of the fays,
Here evermore a hazy brightness plays,
Temples and shining palaces are here,
Majestic porticoes their fronts uprear,

And many a labyrinth and peristyle
The like whereof was never seen erewhile,
Even in Corinth or in Babylon.
Yet let a fairy breathe, and these are gone !
And here, like flickering rays of light, disperse
Through he dim walks of this serene Chartreuse,

The fairies with their knights long since enchanted.
Peace to the aisles by their fair presence haunted !
And now the witch was ready.   First of all,
She lifted high her hands, then let them fall,
While Vincen had like holy Lawrence lain
Upon the porphyry table, mute with pain.

And mightily the spirit of the crone
Appeared to work within her ; and as grown
She seemed, when, rising to her height anew,
She plunged her ladle in the boiling stew
That overflowed the caldron in the heat,
While all the cats arose and ringed her feet,

And, with her left hand, unto Vincen's breast
Applied the scalding drops with solemn zest,
Gazing intently on him where he lay,
Until the cruel hurt was charmed away ;
And all the while, " The Lord is born, is dead,
Is risen, shall rise again," she murmurèd.

Last on the quivering flesh the cross she made
Thrice with her toe-nail ; as in forest glade
A tigress fiercely claws her fallen prey.
And now her speech maketh tumultuous way
To where the dim gates of the future are.
" Yea, he shall rise !   I see him now afar

" Amid the stones and thistles of the hill,
His forehead bleeding heavily.   And still
Over the stones and briers he makes his way,
Bowed by his cross.   Where is Veronica
To wipe the blood ?   And him of Cyrene
To stay him when he fainteth,—where is he ?

" And where the weeping Maries, hair dishevelled ?
All gone !   And rich and poor, before him levelled,
Gaze while he mounts ; and ' Who is this,' one saith,
' Who climbs with shouldered beam, and never stayeth ? '
O carnal sons of men !   The Cross-bearer
Is unto you but as a beaten cur.

" O cruel Jews !   Wherefore so fiercely bite you
The hands that feed, and lick the hands that smite you ?
Receive the fruit of your foul deeds you must.
Your precious gems shall crumble into dust,
And that you deemed fair pulse or wholesome wheat
Shall turn to ashes even while you eat,

" And scare your very hunger.   Woe is me !
Rivers that foam o'er carrion-heaps I see,
And swords and lances in tumultuous motion.
Peace to thy stormy waves, thou vexèd Ocean !
Shall Peter's ancient bark withstand the shock ?
Alas, it strikes upon the senseless rock !

" Nay, but there cometh One with power to save !
Fisher of men, he quells the rebel wave.

A fair new bark the Rhone is entering now :
She hath God's cross uplifted on her prow,
Rainbow divine ! Eternal clemency !
Another land, another sun, I see !

"Dance olive-pickers, where the fruit is shining ;
Drink reapers, on the barley-sheaves reclining !
Revealed by signs so many, God," she said,
" Is in his holy temple worshippèd."
And, stretching forth her hand, the witch of Baux
Pointed the way and bade the children go.

Light gleamed afar. They haste the ray to follow ;
They thread their way to the Cordovan Hollow,
Where sun and air await them, and they seem
To see Mont Majour's wrecks, as in a dream,
Strewn o'er the hill ; yet on the sunlit verge
Pause for one kiss or ever they emerge.

CANTO VII.

The Old Men.

FIXING a troubled eye on the old man,
  Vincen to Master Ambroi thus began,
The while a mighty wind, the poplars bending,
Its howl unto the poor lad's voice was lending :
" I am mad, father, as I oft of late
Have said.   Thinkest thou I'm jesting when I say't ?

Before his nut-shell cot the Rhone beside
Sat Ambroi on a fallen trunk, and plied
His trade.   And, as he peeled the osier withe,
Vincen received it, and, with fingers lithe
And strong, bent the white rods to basket form,
Sitting upon the door-stone.   With the storm

Of wind was the Rhone's bosom agitated,
The waves drove seaward like a herd belated ;
But round about the hut an azure mere
Spread tranquilly.   The billows brake not here :
A pleasant shelter gave the willow-trees,
And beavers gnawed their bitter bark in peace.

While yonder, through the deep of limpid water,
Darted at intervals the dark brown otter,
Following the silver-flashing fish.   Among'
The reeds and willows, pendulines had hung
Their tiny nests, white woven with the wool
Plucked from the poplar when its flowers are full.

And here the small things fluttered full of glee,
Or swang on wind-rocked stems right lazily.
Here, too, a sprightly lassie, golden-haired,—
Head like a crown-cake!—back and forward fared,
And spread on a fig-tree a fishing-net
Unwieldy and with water dripping yet.

Birds, beavers, otters, feared the maid no more
Than whispering reeds or willows of the shore.
This was the daughter of the basket-weaver,
The little Vinceneto. No one ever
Had even bored her ears, poor child! yet so
Her eyes were damson-blue, her bosom low,—

A caper-blossom by the river-side,
Wooed by the splashing of the amorous tide.
But now old Ambroi, with his long white beard
Flowing o'er all his breast, his head upreared,
And answered Vincen's outcry : " What is't ?   Mad ?
You are a blockhead ! that is all, my lad ! "

" Ah ! " said the other, " for the ass to stray,
Sweet must the mead be.   But what do I say?
Thou knowest her !   If she to Arles should fare,
All other maids would hide them in despair ;
For, after her, I think the mould was broken.
And what say to the words herself hath spoken,

" ' You I will have ! ' "—" Why, naught, poor fool ! say I :
Let poverty and riches make reply ! "
" O father ! " Vincen cried, "go, I implore thee,
To Lotus Farm, and tell them all the story !
Tell them to look for virtue, not for gain !
Tell them that I can plough a stony plain,

" Or harrow, or prune vines with any man !
Tell them their six yoke, with my guiding, can

Plough double !   Tell them I revere the old ;
And, if they part us for the sake of gold,
We shall both die, and they may bury us ! "
" Oh, fie !   But you are young who maunder thus,

Quoth Master Ambroi.   " All this talk I know.
The white hen's egg, the chaffinch on the bough,
You'll have the pretty bird this very minute !
Whistle, bring sugared cake, or die to win it ;
Yet will the chaffinch never come, be sure,
And perch upon your finger !   You are poor ! "

" Plague on my poverty ! " poor Vincen cried,
Tearing his hair.   " Is God who hath denied
All that could make life worthy,—is He just ?
And wherefore are we poor?   And wherefore must
We still the refuse of the vineyard gather,
While others pluck the purple clusters rather ? "

Lifting his hands, the old man sternly said,
" Weave on, and drive this folly from your head !
Shall the corn-ears rebuke the reaper, pray ?
Or silly worm to God the Father say,
' Why am I not a star in heaven to shine ? '
Or shall the ox to be a drover pine,

" So to eat corn instead of straw ?   Nay, nay !
Through good and ill we all must hold our way.
The hand's five fingers were unequal made.
Be you a lizard, as your Master bade,
And dwell content upon your wall apart,
And drink your sunbeam with a thankful heart ! "

" I tell thee, father, I this maid adore
More than my sister, than my Maker more ;
And if I have her not, 'tis death, I say ! "
Then to the rough stream Vincen fled away ;
While little Vinceneto burst out weeping,
Let fall her net, and near the weaver creeping,—

"O father ! ere thou drive my brother wild,
Listen to me ! " began the eager child :
" For where I served the master had a daughter ;
And had a labourer, too, who loved and sought her,
Just as our Vincen loves Mirèio.
She was named Alis ; he, Sivèstre : and so

" He laboured like a wolf because he loved.
Skilful and prompt, quiet and saving proved,
And took such care, master slept tranquilly ;
But once—mark, father, how perverse men be!—
One morning master's wife, as it befell,
O'erheard Sivèstre his love to Alis tell.

" So when at dinner all the men were sitting,
The master gave Sivèstre a wrathful greeting.
' Traitor ! ' he cried, with his eyes all aglow,
' You are discovered ! Take your wage, and go ! '
We looked at one another in dismay,
As the good servant rose, and went his way.

" Thereafter, for three weeks, when we were working,
We used to see him round the farmstead lurking,—
A sorry sight ; for all his clothes were torn,
And his face very pale and wild and worn.
And oft at eve he to the trellis came,
And called the little mistress by her name.

" Erelong the hay-rick at its corners four
Burnt all a-flame.   And, father, something more !
They drew a drownèd man out of the well."
Then Ambroi, in gruff tones half-audible,
" A little child a little trouble gives,
And more and more for every year he lives."

Therewith put his long spatterdashes on
Which he himself had made in days bygone,

His hobnailed shoes, and long red cap, and so
Straightway set forth upon the road to Crau.
'Twas harvest-time, the eve of St. John's day,
The hedgerow paths were crowded all the way

With troops of dusty, sunburnt mountaineers
Hired for the reaping of the golden ears.
In fig-wood quivers were their sickles borne,
Slung to a belt across the shoulder worn.
By twos and twos they came, and every pair
Had its own sheaf-binder.   And carts were there,

Bearing the weary elders, and beside
The pipes and tambourines with ribbons tied.
Anon by fields of beardless wheat they passed,
Lashed into billows by the noisy blast;
And "Mon Dieu, but that is noble grain!"
They cried.   "What tufts of ears!   There shall we gain

"Right pleasant reaping!   The wind bows them over;
But see you not how quickly they recover?
Is all the wheat-crop of Provence thus cheering,
Grandfather?" asked a youth, old Ambroi nearing.
"The red is backward still," he made reply;
"But, if this windy weather last, deem I

"Sickles will fail us ere the work be done.
How like three stars the Christmas candles shone!
That was a blessed sign of a good year!"
"Now, grandfather, may the good God thee hear,
And in thy granary the same fulfil!"
So Ambroi and the reapers chatted still

In friendly wise, under the willows wending;
For these as well to Lotus Farm were tending.
It also chanced that Master Ramoun went
That eve to hearken for the wheat's complaint
Against the wind, wild waster of the grain;
And, as he strode over the yellow plain

From north to south, he heard the golden corn
Murmuring, "See the ills that we have borne,
Master, from this great gale.   It spills our seed
And blurs our bloom !"—"Put on your gloves of reed,"
Sang others, "else the ants will be more fleet,
And rob us of our all but hardened wheat.

"When will the sickles come ?"   And Ramoun turned
Toward the trees, and even then discerned
The reapers rising in the distance dim ;
Who, as they nearer drew, saluted him
With waving sickles flashing in the sun.
Then roared the master, "Welcome, every one !

"A very God-send !" cried he, loud and long ;
And soon the sheaf-binders about him throng,
Saying, "Shake hands !   Why, Holy Cross, look here !
What heaps of sheaves, good master, will this year
Cumber your treading-floor !"—"Mayhap," said he :
"We cannot alway judge by what we see.

"Till all is trod, the truth will not be known.
I have known years that promised," he went on,
"Eighty full bushels to the acre fairly,
And yielded in their stead a dozen barely.
Yet let us be content !"   And, with a smile,
He shook their hands all round in friendly style,

And gossiped with old Ambroi affably.
So entered all the homestead path, and he
Called out once more, "Come forth, Mirèio mine :
Prepare the chiccory and draw the wine !"
And she right lavishly the table spread ;
While Ramoun first him seated at its head,

And the rest in their order, for the lunch.
Forthwith the labourers began to crunch

Hard-crusted bread their sturdy teeth between,
And hail the salad made of goats-beard green ;
While fair as an oat-leaf the table shone,
And in superb profusion heaped thereon

Were odorous cheese, onions and garlic hot,
Grilled egg-plant, fiery peppers, and what not,
To sting the palate.   Master Ramoun poured
The wine, king in the field and at the board ;
Raising his mighty flagon now and then,
And calling for a bumper on the men.

" To keep the sickles keen on stony ground,
They must be often whetted, I have found."
The reapers held their goblets, bidden so,
And red and clear the wine began to flow.
" Ay, whet the blades ! " the cheery master cries ;
And furthermore gives order in this wise :

" Now eat your fill, and all your strength restore.
But go thereafter, as you used of yore,
And branches in the copse-wood cut, and bring
In fagots ; thus a great heap gathering.
And when 'tis night, my lads, we'll do the rest !
For this the fête is of Saint John the blest,—

" Saint John the reaper, and the friend of God."
So spake the lord of all these acres broad.
The high and noble art of husbandry,
The rule of men, none better knew than he,
Or how to make a golden harvest grow
From dark sods moistened by the toiler's brow.

A grave and simple master of the soil,
Whose frame was bending now with years and toil ;
Yet oft, of old, when floors were full of wheat,
Glowing with pride he had performed the feat,
Before his youthful corps, upright to stand
Bearing two pecks upon each horny hand.

He could the influence of the moon rehearse ;
Tell when her look is friendly, when adverse ;
When she will raise the sap, and when depress ;
The coming weather from her halo guess,
And from her silver-pale or fiery face.
Clear signs to him were birds and keen March days,

And mouldy bread and noisome August fogs,
St. Clara's dawn, the rainbow-hued sun-dogs,
Wet seasons, times of drought and frost and plenty.
Full oft, in pleasant years, a-ploughing went he,
With six fair, handsome beasts.   And, verily,
Myself have seen, and it was good to see,

The soil part silently before the share,
And its dark bosom to the sun lay bare :
The comely mules, ne'er from the furrow breaking,
Toiled on as though they care and thought were taking
For what they did.   With muzzles low they went,
And arching necks like bows when these are bent,

And hasted not, nor lagged.   Followed along—
Eye on the mules, and on his lips a song—
The ploughman, with one handle only guiding.
So, in the realm where we have seen presiding
Our old friend Ramoun, flourished every thing,
And he bare sceptre like a very king.

Now says he grace, and lifts his eyes above,
And signs the holy cross.   The labourers move
Away to make the bonfire ready.   These
Bring kindling ; those, the boughs of dark pine-trees ;
And the old men alone at table staying,
A silence fell.   But Ambroi brake it, saying,—

" For counsel, Ramoun, am I come to thee ;
For I am in a great perplexity

Thou only canst resolve. Cure see I none.
Thou knowest, Master, that I have a son
Who has been passing good until this day,—
It were ingratitude aught else to say ;

" But there are flaws even in precious stones,
And tender lambs will have convulsions,
And the still waters are perfidious ever :
So my mad boy,—thou wilt believe it never,—
He loves the daughter of a rich freeholder,
And swears he will in his embrace enfold her !

" Ay, swears he will, the maniac !   And his love
And his despair my soul to terror move.
I showed him all his folly, be thou sure,
And how wealth gains, and poverty grows poor
In this hard world.   In vain !   He would but call,
  Cost what it may, tell thou her parents all,—

" ' Tell them to look for virtue, not for gain !
Tell them that I can plough a stony plain,
Or harrow, or prune vines with any man !
Tell them their six yoke, with my guiding, can
Plough double !   Tell them I revere the old ;
And, if they part us for the sake of gold,

" ' We shall both die, and need but burial.'
Now, Master Ramoun, I have told thee all.
Shall I, clad in my rags, for this maid sue,
Or leave my son to die of sorrow ? "—" Whew ! "
The other.   " To such wind spread thou no sail !
Nor he, nor she, will perish of this ail.

" So much, good friend, I say in utmost faith.
Nor would I, Ambroi, fret myself to death
If I were thou ; but, seeing him so mad,
I would say plainly, ' Calm your mind, my lad !
For if you raise a tempest by your passions,
I'll teach you with a cudgel better fashions ! '

" If an ass, Ambroi, for more fodder bray,
Throw him none down, but let thy bludgeon play.
Provençal families in days bygone
Were healthy, brave, and evermore at one,
And strong as plane-trees when a storm befell.
They had their strifes, indeed,—we know it well ;

" But, when returned the holy Christmas eve,
The grandsire all his children would receive
At his own board, under a star-sown tent ;
And ceased the voice of strife and all dissent,
When, lifting hands that wrinkled were and trembled,
He blessed the generations there assembled.

" Moreover, he who is a father truly
Will have his child yield him obedience duly :
The flock that drives the shepherd, soon or late,
Will meet a wolf and a disastrous fate.
When we were young, had any son withstood
His father, he, belike, had shed his blood ! '

" Thou wilt kill me then, father ! It is I
Whom Vincen worships thus despairingly ;
And before God and our most holy Mother,
I give my soul to him, and to no other ! "
A deathlike hush followed Mirèio's word.
The wife of Ramoun was the first who stirred.

Upspringing with clasped hands and utterance wild,
" Your speech is an atrocious insult, child !
Your love's a thorn that long hath stung us deep.
Alari, the owner of a thousand sheep,
You sent away ; and keeper Veran too,
Disgusted with your scorn, his suit withdrew ;

" Also the wealthy herdsman, Ourrias,
You treated as a dog and a scapegrace !

Tramp through the country with your beggar, then !
Herd with strange women and with outcast men !
And cook your pot with fortune-telling crones
Under a bridge mayhap, upon three stones.

"Go, gypsy, you are free !" the mother said ;
Nor stayed Ramoun her pitiless tirade,
Though his eye like a taper burned.   But now
The lightning flashed under his shaggy brow,
And his wrath brake, all barriers overbearing,
Like swollen torrent down a mountain tearing.

" Your mother's right ! " he said.   " Go ! travel yonder,
And take the tempest with you where you wander !
Nay, but you shall not !   Here you shall remain,
Though I should bind you with an iron chain,
Or hold like a rebellious jumart, look !
Dragged by the nostrils with an iron hook !

"Yea, though you pine with sickly melancholy,
Till from your cheeks the roses perish wholly,
Or fade as snow fades when the sun is hot
On the hill-sides in spring, go shall you not ! '
And mark, Mirèio !   Sure as the hearth's ashes
Rest on that brick, and sure as the Rhone dashes

" Above its banks when it is overfull,
And sure as that's a lamp, and here I rule,
You'll see him never more ! "   The table leapt
Beneath his fist.   Mirèio only wept.
Her heavy tears like dew on smallage rain,
Or grapes o'er ripe before a hurricane.

" And who," resumed the old man, blind with rage,—
" Curse it !—I say, who, Ambroi, will engage
Thou didst not with the younger ruffian plot
This vile abduction, yonder in thy cot ? "
Then Ambroi also sprang infuriate,—
" Good God ! " he cried, " we are of low estate ;

" But let me tell you that our hearts are high !
No shame, no stain, is honest poverty !
I've served my country forty years or more
On shipboard, and I know the cannon's roar,
So young that I could scarce a boat-hook swing
When on my first cruise I went wandering.

" I've seen Melinda's empire far away,
And with Suffren have haunted India,
And done my duty over all the world
In the great wars, where'er our flag unfurled
That southern chief who passed his conquering hand
With one red sweep from Spain to Russian land,

" And at whose drum-beat every clime was quaking
Like aspen-tree before the tempest shaking ;
Horrors of boarding, shipwreck's agonies,—
These have I known, and darker things than these,
Days than the sea more bitter.   Being poor,
No bit of motherland might I secure.

" Scorned of the rich, I might not dress the sward,
But suffer forty years without reward.
We ate dog's food, on the hoar-frost we lay :
Weary of life, we rushed into the fray,
And so upbore the glorious name of France.
But no one holds it in remembrance ! "

His caddis-cloak upon the ground he threw,
And spake no more.   " What great thing wilt thou do ? "
Asked Ramoun, and his tone was full of scorn.
" I, too, have heard the cannon-thunder borne
Along the valley of Toulon, have seen
The bridge of Arcole stormed, and I have been

" In Egypt when her sands were red with gore ;
But we, like men, when those great wars were o'er,

F

Returning, fiercely fell upon the soil,
And dried our very marrow up with toil
The day began long ere the eastern glow,
The rising moon surprised us at the hoe.

"They say the Earth is generous.   It is true !
But, like a nut-tree, naught she gives to you
Unless well-beaten.   And if all were known,
Each clod of landed ease thus hardly won,
He who should number them would also know
The sweat-drops that have fallen from my brow.

"And must I, by Ste. Anne of Apt, be still?
Like satyr toil, of siftings eat my fill,
That all the homestead may grow wealthy, and
Myself before the world with honour stand,
Yet go and give my daughter to a tramp,
A vagabond, a straw-loft-sleeping scamp?

"God's thunder strike you and your dog !   Begone !
But I," the master said, "will keep my swan."
These were his last rough words ; and steadily
Ambroi arose, and his cloak lifted he,
And only rested on his staff to say,
"Adieu !   Mayst thou not regret this day !

"And may the good God and his angels guide
The orange-laden bark across the tide !"
Then, as he passed into the falling night,
From the branch-heap arose a ruddy light,
And one long tongue of flame the wanderer sees,
Curled like a horn by the careering breeze ;

And round it reapers dancing blithesomely,
With pulsing feet, and haughty heads and free
Thrown back, and faces by the bonfire lit,
Loud crackling as the night-wind fanneth it.
The sound of coals that to the brazier fall
Blends with the fife-notes fine but musical,

And merry as the song of the hedge-sparrow.
Ah, but it thrills the old Earth to her marrow
When thou dost visit her, beloved St. John !
The sparks went whirling upward, and hummed on
The tabor gravely and incessantly,
Like the low surging of a tranquil sea.

Then did the dusky troop their sickle wave,
And three great leaps athwart the flame they gave,
And cloves of odorous garlic from a string
Upon the glowing embers they did fling,
And holy herb and John's-wort bare anigh ;
And these were purified and blessed thereby.

Then "Hail, St. John !" thrice rose a deafening shout ;
And hills and plain, illumined round about,
Sparkled as though the dark were showering stars.
And sure the Saint, above the heaven's blue bars,
The breath of all this incense doth inhale,
Wafted aloft by the unconscious gale.

CANTO VIII.

La Crau.

THE rage of the mighty lioness
    Who shall restrain?
She came to her den, and she found it bare :
A Moorish huntsman had entered there.
The huntsman came, and the whelp is gone.
Away through the canebrake they have flown,
Galloping far at a headlong pace.
        To follow—vain !
She roars awhile in her deep despite,
Then rises and courses, lank and light,
Over the hills of Barbary.
As a maid bereft of her love is she.

Mirèio lay upon her little bed,
Clasping in both her hands her burning head.
Dim was the chamber ; for the stars alone
Saw the maid weep, and heard her piteous moan,—
" Help, Mother Mary, in my sore distress !
Oh, cruel fate ! Oh, father pitiless,

" Who tread me underfoot! Could you but see
My heart's mad tumult, you would pity me !
You used to call me darling long ago,
And now you bend me to the yoke as though
I were a vicious colt that you were fain
To break. Why does the sea not flood this plain ?

"I would the wealthy lands that make me weep
Were hid for evermore in the great deep !
Ah, had I in a serpent's hole been born,
Of some poor vagrant, I were less forlorn !
For then if any lad, my Vincen even,
Had asked my hand, mayhap it had been given.

"O Vincen, who so handsome are and true !
If only they would let me go to you,
I'd cling as clings the tender ivy-vine
Unto the oak : I would not ever pine
For food, but life in your caresses find,
And drink at wayside pools with happy mind."

So on her pallet the sweet maid lay sobbing,
Fire in her heart and every vein a-throbbing,
And all the happy time remembering—
Oh, calm and happy !—of her love's fair spring,
Until a word in Vincen's very tone
Comes to her memory.   "'Twas you, my own,—

"'Twas you," she cried, " came one day to the farm,
And said, 'If ever thou dost come to harm,—
If any lizard, wolf, or poisonous snake,
Ever should wound thee with its fang,—betake
Thyself forthwith to the most holy Saints,
Who cure all ills and hearken all complaints.'

"And sure I am in trouble now," she said :
"Therefore we'll go, and come back comforted."
Then lightly from her white cot glided she,
And straightway opened, with a shining key,
The wardrobe where her own possessions lay :
It was of walnut wood, and carven gay.

Here were her childhood's little treasures all :
Here sacredly she kept the coronal

Worn at her first communion; and thereby
A faded sprig of lavender and dry,
And a wax taper almost burned, as well,
Once blessed, the distant thunder to dispel.

A smart red petticoat she first prepares,
Which she herself had quilted into squares,—
Of needlework a very masterpiece;
And round her slender waist she fastens this;
And over it another, finer one
She draws; and next doth a black bodice don,

And fasten firmly with a pin of gold.
On her white shoulders, her long hair unrolled,
Curling, and loose like a dark garment, lay,
Which, gathering up, she swiftly coils away
Under a cap of fine, transparent lace;
Then decks the veilèd tresses with all grace,

Thrice with a ribbon blue encircling them,—
The fair young brow's Arlesian diadem.
Lastly, she adds an apron to the rest,
And folds a muslin kerchief o'er her breast.
In her dire haste, alone, the child forgat
The shallow-crowned, broad-brimmed Provençal hat,

That might have screened her from the mortal heat.
But, so arrayed, crept forth on soundless feet
Adown the wooden staircase, in her hand
Her shoes, undid the heavy door-bar, and
Her soul unto the watchful saints commended,
As away like a wind of night she wended.

It was the hour when constellations keep
Their friendly watch o'er followers of the deep.
The eye of St. John's eagle flashed afar,
As it alighted on a burning star,
One of the three where the evangelist
Hath his alternate dwelling.   Cloud nor mist

Defaced the dark serene of star-lit sky ;
But the great chariot of souls went by
On wingèd wheels along the heavenly road,
Bearing away from earth its blessed load.
Far up the shining steeps of Paradise,
The circling hills behold it as it flies.

Mirèio hasted no less anxiously
Than Magalouno in the days gone by,
Who searched the wood with sad, inquiring glance
For her lost lover, Pèire of Provence,
When cruel waves divorced him from her side,
And left her lone and wretched.   Soon espied

The maid, upon the boundary of the lea,
Folds where her sire's own shepherds could she see
Already milking.   Some the sheep compelled,
Against the pen-side by the muzzle held,
To suckle quietly their tawny lambs.
Always arose the bleat of certain dams ;

While other childless ones the shepherds guide
Toward the milker.   On a stone astride,
Mute as the very night, sits he, and dim ;
While, pressed from swollen udders, a long stream
Of warm fine milk into the pail goes leaping,
The white froth high about its border creeping.

The sheep-dogs all in tranquil slumber lay.
The fine, large dogs—as white as lilies they—
Stretched round the enclosure, muzzles deep in thyme.
And peace was everywhere, and summer clime ;
And o'er the balmy country, far and near,
Brooded a heaven full of stars, and clear.

So in the stillness doth Mirèio dash
Along the hurdles, like a lightning flash,

Lifting a wailing cry that never varies,—
" Will none go with me to the holy Maries,
Of all the shepherds?" They and the sheep hear it,
And see the maiden flitting like a spirit,

And huddle up, and bow their heads, as though
Smit by a sudden gale. The farm-dogs know
Her voice, but never stir her flight to stay.
And now is she already far away,
Threads the dwarf-oaks, and like a partridge rushes
Over the holly and the camphyre bushes,

Her feet scarce touching earth. And now she passes
Curlews in flocks asleep amid the grasses
Under the oaks, who, roused from slumber soft,
Arise in haste, and wing their flight aloft
Over the sad and barren plain ; and all
Together " Cour'li ! cour'li ! cour'li !" call,

Until the Dawn, with her dew-glittering tresses,
From mountain-top to level slow progresses,
Sweetly saluted by the tufted lark,
Soaring and singing o'er the caverns dark
In the great hills, whose pinnacles each one
Appear to sway before the rising sun.

Then was revealed La Crau, the bare, the waste,
The rough with stones, the ancient, and the vast,
Whose proud old giants, if the tale be true,
Once dreamed, poor fools, the Almighty to subdue
With but a ladder and their shoulders brave ;
But He them 'whelmed in a destroying wave.

Already had the rebels dispossest
The Mount of Victory of his tall crest,
Lifted with lever from its place ; and sure
They would have helped it high upon Ventour,
As they had piled the rugged escarpment
They from the Alpine range had earlier rent.

But God his hand extended o'er the plain :
The north-west wind, thunder, and hurricane
He loosed ; and these arose like eagles three
From mountain clefts and caverns and the sea,
Wrapped in thick fog, with fury terrible,
And on the marble pile together fell.

Then were the rude Colossi overthrown ;
And a dense covering of pudding-stone
Spread o'er La Crau, the desolate, the vast,
The mute, the bare to every stormy blast ;
Who wears the hideous garment to this day.
Meanwhile Mirèio farther speeds away

From the home-lands, while the sun's ardent glare
Makes visible all round the shimmering air ;
And shrill cicalas, grilling in the grass,
Beat madly evermore their tiny brass.
Nor tree for shade was there, nor any beast :
The many flocks, that in the winter feast.

On the short, savoury grasses of the moor,
Had climbed the Alps, where airs are cool and pure,
And pastures fadeless.   Yet the maid doth fly
Under the pouring fire of a June sky,—
Fly, fly, like lightning.   Lizards large and gray
Peep from their holes, and to each other say,

" She must be mad who thus the shingle clears,
Under a heat that sets the junipers
A-dancing on the hills ; on Crau, the sands."
The praying mantes lift beseeching hands,
" Return, return, O pilgrim ! " murmuring,
" For God hath opened many a crystal spring ;

" And shady trees hath planted, so the rose
To save upon your cheeks.   Why, then, expose
F*

Your brow to the unpitying summer heat
Vainly as well the butterflies entreat.
For her the wings of love, the wind of faith,
Bear on together, as the tempest's breath

White gulls astray over the briny plains
Of Agui-Morto. Utter sadness reigns
In scattered sheep-cots of their tenants left,
And overrun with salicorne. Bereft
In the hot desert, seemed the maid to wake,
And see nor spring nor pool her thirst to slake,

And slightly shuddered. "Great St. Gent!" she cried,
"O hermit of the Bausset mountain-side!
O fair young labourer, who to thy plough
Didst harness the fierce mountain-wolf ere now,
And in the flinty rock, recluse divine,
Didst open springs of water and of wine,

"And so revive thy mother, perishing
Of heat! like me, when they were slumbering,
Thou didst forsake thy household, and didst fare
Alone with God through mountain-passes, where
Thy mother found thee! For me, too, dear Saint,
Open a spring; for I am very faint,

"And my feet by the hot stones blisterèd!"
Then, in high heaven, heard what Mirèio said
The good St. Gent: and soon she doth discover
A well far off, with a bright stone laid over;
And, like a marten through a shower of rain,
Speeds through the flaming sun-rays, this to gain.

The well was old, with ivy overrun—
A watering-place for flocks; and from the sun
Scarce by it sheltered sat a little boy,
With basket-full of small white snails for toy.
With his brown hands, he one by one withdrew them,
The tiny harvest-snails; and then sang to them,—

"Snaily, snaily, little nun,
Come out of the cell, come into the sun!
Show me your horns without delay,
Or I'll tear your convent-walls away."

Then the fair maid of Crau, when she had dipped
Her burning lips into the pail, and sipped,
Quickly upraised a lovely, rosy face,
And, "Little one! what dost thou here?" she says.
A pause. "Pick snailies from the stones and grass?"
"Thou hast guessed right!" the urchin's answer was.

"Here in my basket have I—see, how many!
Nuns, harvest-snails, and these, as good as any!"
"And thou dost eat them"—"Nay, not I," replied he;
"But mother carries them to Arles on Friday,
And sells them; and brings back nice, tender bread.
Thou wilt have been to Arles?"—"Never!" she said.

"What, never been to Arles! But I've been there!
Ah, poor young lady! Couldst thou see how fair
And large a city that same Arles is grown!
She covers all the seven mouths of the Rhone.
Upon the islands of the great salt-mere
Her cattle graze: wild horses doth she rear.

"And in one summer, corn enough doth grow,
To feed her seven full years, if need were so.
She's fishermen who fish on every sea,—
Seamen who front the storms right valiantly
Of distant waters." Thus with pretty pride
The boy his sunny country glorified,

In golden speech;—her blue and heaving ocean;
Her Mont Majour, that keeps the mills in motion,—
These with soft olives ever feeding fully;
Her bitterns in the marshes booming dully.
One thing alone, thou lovely, dusky town,
The child forgat,—of all thy charms the crown:

He said not, fruitful Arles, that thy fine air
Gives to thy daughters beauty rich and rare,
As grapes to autumn, or as wings to bird,
Or fragrance to the hill-sides.   Him had heard
The country maiden, sadly, absently.
But now, " Bright boy, wilt thou not go with me ? "

She said ; " for, ere the frogs croak in the willow,
My foot must planted be beyond the billow.
Come with me !   I must o'er the Rhone be rowed,
And left there in the keeping of my God ! "
" Now, then," the urchin cried, " thou poor, dear lady,
Thou art in luck ! for we are fishers," said he ;

" And thou shalt sleep under our tent this night,
Pitched in the shadow of the poplars white,
So keeping all thy pretty clothing on ;
And father, with the earliest ray of dawn,
In our own little boat will put thee o'er ! "
But she, " Do not detain me, I implore :

" I am yet strong enough this night to wander."
" Now God forbid ! " was the lad's prompt rejoinder :
" Wouldst thou see, then, the crowd of sorry shapes
From the Trau-de-la-Capo that escapes ?
For if they meet thee, be thou sure of this, —
They'll drag thee with them into the abyss ! "

" Trau-de-la-Capo !   What may that be, pray ? "
" I'll tell thee, lady, as we pick our way
Over the stones."   And forthwith he began :
" Once was a treading-floor that overran
With wealth of sheaves.   To-morrow, on thy ways,
Thou'lt pass, upon the riverside, the place.

' Trod by a circle of Camargan steeds,
The tall sheaves have been yielding up their sceds

To the incessant hoofs, a month or more.
No pause, no rest ; and, on the treading-floor,
Dusty and winding, still the eye perceives
A very mountain of untrodden sheaves.

" Also, the weather was so fiercely hot,
The floor would burn like fire ; and rested not
The wooden forks that more sheaves yet supplied
While at the horses' muzzles there were shied
Clusters of bearded ears unceasingly,—
They flew as arrows from the cross-bow fly.

" And on St. Peter's day and on St. Charles'
Rang, and rang vainly, all the bells of Arles :
There was no Sunday and no holiday
For the unhappy horses : but alway
The heavy tramp around the weary road,
Alway the pricking of the keeper's goad,

" Alway the orders issued huskily,
As in the fiery whirlwind still stood he.
The greedy master of the treaders white
Had even muzzled them, in his despite.
And, when Our Lady's day in August came,
The coupled beasts were treading, all the same,

" The pilèd sheaves, foam-drenched. Their livers clung
Fast to their ribs, and their jaws drivelling hung,
When suddenly an icy, northern gale
Smit, swept the floor,—and God's blasphemers pale.
It quakes ! It parts ! On a black caldron's brink
Now stand they, and their eyes with horror sink.

" Then the sheaves whirl with fury terrible.
Pitch-forkers, keepers, keepers-aids as well,
Struggle to save them ; but they naught can do :
The van, the van-goats, and the mill-stones too,
Horses and drivers, treading-floor, and master
Are swallowed up in one immense disaster ! "

"You make me shudder!" poor Mirèio said.
"Ah, but that is not all, my pretty maid!
Thou thinkest me a little mad, may be:
But on the morrow thou the spot wilt see;
And carp and tench in the blue water playing,
And, in the reeds, marsh-blackbirds roundelaying.

"But on Our Lady's day, when mounts again
The fire-crowned sun to the meridian,
Lay thee down softly, ear to earth," said he,
"And eye a-watch, and presently thou'lt see
The gulf, at first so limpid, will begin
To darken with the shadow of the sin;

"And slowly up from the unquiet deep
A murmuring sound, like buzzing flies, will creep;
And then a tinkling, as of tiny bells,
That soon into an awful uproar swells
Among the water-weeds!   Like human voices
Inside an amphora the fearsome noise is!

"And then it is the trot of wasted horses
Painfully tramping round their weary courses
Upon a hard, dry surface, evermore
Echoing like a summer threshing-floor,
Whom drives a brutal keeper, nothing loth,
And hurries them with insult and with oath.

"But, when the holy sun is sinking low,
The blasphemies turn hoarse and fainter grow,
The tinkling dies among the weeds.   Far off,
The limping, sorry steed is heard to cough;
And, on the top of the tall reeds a-swinging,
Once more the blackbirds begin sweetly singing."

So, full of chat, and with his basket laden,
Travelled the little man before the maiden;

While the descending sun with rose invests
The great blue ramparts and the golden crests
Of the hill-range, peaceful and pure and high,
Blending its outline with the evening sky.

Seemed the great orb, as he withdrew in splendour,
God's peace unto the marshes to surrender,
And to the great lake, and the olives gray
Of the Vaulungo, and the Rhone away
There in the distance, and the reapers weary,
Who now unbend, and quaff the sea-air, cheery.

Till the boy cries that far away he sees
The home-tent's canvas fluttering in the breeze.
" And the white poplar, dear maid, seest thou ?
And brother Not, who climbs it even now ?
He's there after cicalas, be thou sure ;
Or to spy me returning o'er the moor.

" Ah, now he sees us !   And my sister Zeto,
Who helped him with her shoulder, turns this way too ;
And seems to tell my mother that she may
Put on the *bouillabaise* without delay.
And mother also, I can see her leaning
Over the boat, and the fresh fish a-gleaning."

Then, as the two made haste with one accord
To mount the dike, the lusty fisher roared,
" Now this is charming !   Look this way, my wife !
Our little Andreloun, upon my life,
Will be the prince of fishers one day," said he ;
" For he has caught the queen of eels already ! "

CANTO IX.

The Muster.

ALL sorrowfully droop the lotus-trees ;
  And heart-sick to their hives withdraw the bees,
Forgetful of the heath with savoury sweet,
And with milk-thistle.   Water-lilies greet
Kingfishers blue that to the vivary hie,
And " Have you seen Mirèio?" is their cry.

While Ramoun and his wife by the fireside
Are sitting, lost in grief, and swollen-eyed,
And at their hearts the bitterness of death.
" Doubtless," they said, " her reason wandereth.
Oh, what a mad and wretched maid it is !
Oh, what a heavy, cruel downfall this !

" Oh, dire disgrace !   Our beauty and our hope
So with the last of trampers to elope !
Fled with a gypsy !   And who shall discover
The secret hole of this kidnapping lover,
Where he the shameless one concealèd hath? "
And, as they spake, they knit their brows in wrath.

Now came the cupbearer with ass and pannier,
And from the threshold, in his wonted manner,
" Good-morrow," Jane.   "I'm come," he said, " to seek
The labourer's lunch."   And Ramoun could but wreak
His anguish on him.   " Go, you cursèd churl !
I'm as a cork-tree barked, without my girl ! "

" Yet hark ye, cupbearer, upon your track
Across the fields like lightning go you back,
And bid the ploughmen and the mowers all
Quit ploughs and scythes, the harvesters let fall
Their sickles, and their shepherds too," said he,
" Forsake their flocks, and instant come to me ! "

Then, fleeter than a goat, the faithful man
O'er stony fallow and red clover ran,
Threaded holm-oaks on long declivities,
Leaped o'er the roads along the base of these,
And now already scents the sweet perfume
Of new-mown hay, and the blue-tufted bloom

Of tall lucerne descries ; and presently
The measured sweep of the long scythes hears he,
And lusty mowers bending in a row
Beholds, and grass by the keen steel laid low
In verdant swaths,—ever a pleasant sight,—
And children, and young maidens, with delight

Raking the hay and in cocks piling it ;
While crickets, that before the mowers flit,
Hark to their singing.   Also, farther on,
An ash-wood cart, by two white oxen drawn,
Where a deft cartman, piles the well-cured grass
By armfuls high and higher, till the mass

Rises about his loins, and so conceals
The rails, the cart-beam, and the very wheels ;
And, when the cart moves on, with the hay trailing,
It seems like some unwieldy vessel sailing.
But now the cartman rises, and descries
The runner, and " Hold, men ! there's trouble ! " cries ;

And all his aids, who in great forkfuls carry
To him the hay, do for a moment tarry,

And wipe their streaming brows ; and mowers rest
The scythe-back carefully upon the breast,
And whet the edge, as they the plain explore
That Phœbus wings his burning arrows o'er.

Began the rustic messenger straightway,
" Hear men, what our good master bade me say :
" ' Cupbearer,' was his word, ' upon your track
Across the fields like lightning go you back,
And bid the ploughmen and the mowers all
Quit ploughs and scythes, the harvesters let fall

" ' Their sickles, and the shepherds hastily
Forsake their flocks, and hither come to me ! ' "
Then, fleeter than a goat, the faithful man
O'er the rich, madder-growing hillocks ran,—
Althen's bequest,—and saw on every hand
The gold of perfect ripeness tinge the land,

And centaury-starred fields, and ploughmen bent
Above their ploughs and on their mules intent,
And earth, awakened from her winter-sleep,
And shapeless clods upturned from furrows deep,
And wagtails frisking o'er ; and yet again,
" Hearken to what our master saith, good men !

" ' Cupbearer,' was his word, ' upon your track
Across the fields like lightning go you back,
And bid the ploughmen and the mowers all
Quit ploughs and scythes, the harvesters let fall
Their sickles, and the shepherds hastily
Forsake their flocks, and hither come to me ! ' "

Then the stout runner, fleeter than the goats,
Dashed through the pieces waving with wild-oats,
Fosses o'erleaped with meadow-flowers bright,
And in great yellow wheat-fields passed from sight,
Where reapers forty, sickle each in hand,
Like a devouring fire fall on the land,

And strip her mantle rich and odorous
From off her breast, and, ever gaining thus
As wolves upon their prey, rob, hour by hour,
Earth of her gold, and summer of her flower ;
While in the wake of each, in ordered line,
Falls the loose grain, like tendrils of the vine.

And the sheaf-binders, ever on the watch,
The dropping wheat in handfuls deftly catch,
And underneath the arm the same bestow
Until, so gathering, they have enow ;
When, pressing with the knee, they tightly bind,
And lastly fling the perfect sheaf behind.

Twinkle the sickles keen like swarming bees,
Or laughing ripple upon sunny seas
Where flounders are at play.   Erect and tall,
With rough beards blent, in heaps pyramidal,
The sheaves by hundreds rise.   The plain afar
Shows like a tented camp in days of war ;

Even like that which once arose upon
Our own Beaucaire, in days how long withdrawn !
When came a host of terrible invaders,
The great Simon, and all the French crusaders,
Led by a legate, and in fierce advance
Count Raymond slaughtered and laid waste Provence.

And here, with gleanings falling from her fingers,
Full many a merry gleaner strays and lingers ;
Or in the warm lea of the stacks of corn,
Or 'mid the canes, drops languidly, o'erborne
By some long look, that e'en bewilders her,
Because Love also is a harvester.

And yet again the master's word,—" Go back
Like lightning, cupbearer, upon your track,

And bid the ploughmen and the mowers all
Quit ploughs and scythes, the harvesters let fall
Their sickles, and the shepherds instantly
Forsake their flocks, and hither come to me ! "

Then fleeter than a goat sped on his way
The faithful soul, straight through the olives gray,
On, on, like a north-eastern gale descending
Upon the vineyards, and the branches rending,
Until, away in Crau, the waste, the lonely,
Behold him, where the partridge whirreth only ;

And, still remote, discovers he the flocks
Tranquilly lying under the dwarf-oaks,
And the chief-shepherd, with his helpers young,
For noon-tide rest about the heather flung,
And little wagtails hopping at their ease
O'er sheep that ruminate unmoved by these.

And slowly, slowly sailing o'er the sea
Diaphanous vapours, light and white, sees he,
And deems that up in heaven some fair saint,
Gliding too near the sun, is stricken faint
On the aerial heights, and hath let fall
Her convent-veil.   And still the herald's call :—

" Hark, shepherds, to the master's word,—' Go back
Like lightning, cupbearer, upon your track,
And bid the ploughmen and the mowers all
Quit ploughs and scythes, the reapers too let fall
Their sickles, and the shepherds instantly
Forsake their flocks, and hither come to me ! "

Then the scythes rested and the ploughs were stayed,
The forty highland reapers each his blade
Let fall, and rushed as bees on new-found wings
Forsake the hive, begin their wanderings,
And, by the din of clanging cymbals led,
Gather them to a pine.   So also fled

The labourers one and all ; the waggoners,
And they who tended them ; the rick-builders,
Gleaners, and shepherds, and of sheaves the heapers,
Binders of sheaves, rakers, mowers, and reapers,
Mustered them at the homestead.   There, heart-sore
And silent, on the grass-grown treading-floor,

The master and his wife sat down to bide
The coming of the hands ; who, as they hied
Thither, much marvelled at the strange behest
So calling them from toil, and who addrest
These words unto old Ramoun, drawing near :
" Thou sentest for us, master.   We are here."

Then Ramoun raised his head, and thus replied :
" The great storm alway comes at harvest-tide.
However well-advised, as we advance
We must, poor souls, all stumble on mischance :
I cannot say it plainer.   Friends, I pray,
Let each tell what he knows, without delay ! "

Lauren de Gout came forward first.   Now he
Had failed no single year since infancy
His quivered sickle from the hills to bring
Down into Arles when ears were yellowing.
Brown as a church-stone, he, with weather-stain,
Or ancient rock the sea-waves charge in vain.

The sun might scorch, the north-west wind might roar,
But this old king of reapers evermore
Was first at work.   And now with him there came
Seven rough and stalwart boys who bore his name.
Him with one voice the harvesters did make
Their chief, and justly : therefore thus he spake :

" If it be true that, when the dawning sky
Is ruddy, there is rain or snow close by,

Then what I saw this very morn, my master,
Presageth surely sorrow and disaster.
So may God stay the earthquake ! But as night
Fled westward, followed by the early light,

"And wet with dew as ever, I the men
First summoned briskly to their toil again,
And then myself, my sleeves uprolling gayly,
Bent me to mine own task, as I do daily ;
But at the first stroke wounded thus my hand,—
A thing which hath not happened, understand,

"For thirty years." His fingers then he showed,
And the deep gash, wherefrom the blood yet flowed.
Then groaned, more piteously than before,
Mirèio's parents ; while a lusty mower,
One Jan Bouquet, a knight of La Tarasque
From Tarascon, a hearing rose to ask.

A rough lad he, yet kind and comely too.
None with such grace in Condamino threw
The pike and flag, and never merrier fellow
Sang Lagadigadèu's ritournello
About the gloomy streets of Tarascon,
When, once a year, they ring with shout and song,

And brighten up with dances and are blithe.
He might have been a master of the scythe,
Could he have held the straight, laborious path ;
But, when the fête-days came, farewell the swath,
And welcome revels underneath the trees,
And orgies in the vaulted hostelries,

And bull-baitings, and never-ending dances !
A very roisterer he who now advances,
With, "As we, master, in long sweeps were mowing,
I hailed a nest of francolines, just showing
Under a tuft of tares ; and, as I bent
Over the pendent grass, with the intent

" To count the fluttering things, what do I see
But horrible red ants—oh, misery !—
In full possession of the nest and young !
Three were then dead.   The rest, with vermin stung,
Their little heads out of the nest extended,
As though, poor things, they cried to be defended ;

" But a great cloud of ants, more venemous
Than nettles, greedy, eager, furious,
Them were o'erwhelming even then ; and I,
Leaning upon my scythe right pensively,
Could hear, far off, the mother agonize
Over their cruel fate, with piteous cries."

This tale of woe, following upon the other,
Is a lance-thrust to father and to mother :
The worst foreboding seemeth justified.
Then, as a tempest in the hot June-tide,
Gathering silently, ascends the air,
The weather darkening ever, till the glare

Of lightning shows in the north-east, and loud
Peal follows peal, another left the crowd,
One Lou Marran.   It was a name renowned
In all the farms when winter-eves came round,
And labourers, chatting while the mules were stalled
And pulling lucerne from the rack, recalled

What things befell when first this man was hired,
Until the lights for lack of oil expired.
Seed-time it was, and every other man
Was opening up his furrow save Marran ;
Who, hanging back, eyed coulter, tackle, share,
As he the like had seen not anywhere.

Till the chief-ploughman spake : " Here is a lout
To plough for hire !   Why, a hog with his snout

I wager would work better !"—" I will take
Thy bet," said Lou Marran ; " and be the stake
Three golden louis ! Either thou or I,
Master, that sum will forfeit presently."

" Let blow the trumpet !"   Then the ploughmen twain
In two unswerving lines upturn the plain,
Making for the chosen goal,—two poplars high.
The sun-rays gild the ridges equally,
And all the labourers call out, " Well done !
Thy furrow, chieftain, is a noble one ;

" Yet, sooth to say, so straight the other is,
One might an arrow shoot the length of this."
And Lou Marran was winner,—he who here
Before the baffled council doth appear,
All pale, his bitter evidence to bear :
" Comrades, as I was whistling, at my share,

" Not long ago, methought the land was rough,
And we would stretch, the day to finish off ;
When, lo ! my beasts with fear began to quake,
Bristled their hairy sides, their ears lay back.
They stopped ; and, with dazed eyes, I saw all round
The field-herbs fade, and wither to the ground.

" I touch my pair.   Baiardo sadly eyes
His master, but stirs not.   Falet applies
His nostril to the furrow.   Then I lash
Their shins ; and, all in terror, off they dash,
So that the ash-wood beam—the beam, I say—
Is rent, and yoke and tackle borne away.

" Then grew I pale, and all my breath was gone ;
And, seized as with a strong convulsion,
I ground my jaws.   A dreadful shudder grew
Upon me,—and my hair upraised, I knew,
As thistle-down is raised by the wind's breath ;
But the wind sweeping over me was Death."

" Mother of God ! " Mirèio's mother cried
In torture, " do thou in thy mantle hide
Mine own sweet child ! " and on her knees she dropped
With lifted eyes and parted lips : yet stopped
Ere any word was spoken, for she saw
Antéume, shepherd-chief and milker, draw

Hurriedly toward them. " And why," he was panting,
" Was she the junipers untimely haunting ? "
Then, the ring entering, his tale he told.
" This morn, as we were milking in the fold,—
So early that above the bare plain showed
The sky yet hob-nailed with the stars of God,—

" A soul, a shadow, or a spectre swept
Across the way. The dogs all silence kept,
As if afraid, and the sheep huddled close.
Thought I,—who scarce have time, as master knows,
Ever an *Ave* in the church to offer,—
' Speak, soul, if thou art blest. If not, go suffer ! '

" Then came a voice I knew,—it never varies,—
' Will none go with me to the holy Maries,
Of all the shepherds ? ' Ere the word was said,
Afar over the plain the voice had fled.
Wilt thou believe it, master ?—it was she,
Mirèio ! " Cried the people, " Can it be ? "

" It was herself ! " the shepherd-chief replied :
" I saw her in the star-light past me glide,
Not, surely, as she was in other days,
But lifting up a wan, affrighted face ;
Whereby she was a living soul, I knew,
And stung by some exquisite anguish too."

At this dread word, the labourers groan, and wring
Each other's horny palms. " But who will bring,"

The stricken mother began wildly shrieking,
" *Me* to the saints ?   My bird I must be seeking !
My partridge of the stony field," she said,
" I must o'ertake, wherever she has fled.

" And if the ants attack her, then these teeth
Shall grind them and their hill ! If greedy Death
Dare touch my darling rudely, then will I
Break his old, rusty scythe, and she shall fly
Away across the jungle ! "   Crying thus,
Jano Mario fled delirious

Back to the home ; while Ramoun order gave,
" Cartman, set up the cart-tilt, wet the nave,
And oil the axle, and without delay
Harness Moureto.   We go far to-day,
And it is late."   The mother, in despair,
Mounted the cart ; and more and more the air

Resounded with the transports of her woe :
"O pretty dear !   O wilderness of Crau !
O endless, briny plains ! O dreadful sun,
Be kind, I pray you, to the fainting one !
But for her,—the accursèd witch Taven,—
Who lured my darling into her foul den,

And poured before her, as I know right well,
Her philters and her potions horrible,
And made her drink,—now may the demons all
Who lured St. Anthony upon her fall,
And drag her body o'er the rocks of Baux ! "
As the unhappy soul lamented so,

Her tones were smothered by the cart's rude shaking ;
And the farm-labourers, a last look taking
To see if none were coming o'er the plain,
Turned slowly, sadly, to their toil again ;
While swarms of gnats, the idle, happy things,
Filled the green walks with sound of humming wings.

CANTO X.

Camargue.

L ISTEN to me, good people of Provence,
  Countrymen one and all, from Arles to Vence,
From Vanensolo even to Marseilles,
And, if the heat oppress you, come, I pray,
To Durancolo banks, and, lying low,
Hear the maid's tale, and weep the lover's woe!

The little boat, in Andreloun's control,
Parted the water silent as a sole,
The while the enamoured maiden whom I sing,
Herself on the great Rhone adventuring,
Beside the urchin sat, and scanned the wave
Intently, with a dreamy eye and grave,

Till the boy-boatman spake : " Now knewest thou ever,
Young lady, how immense is the Rhone river?
Betwixt Camargue and Crau might holden be
Right noble jousts ! That is Camargue ! " said he ;
" That isle so vast it can discern, I deem,
All the seven mouths of the Arlesian stream."

The rose-lights of the morn were beauteous
Upon the river, as he chatted thus.
And the tartanes, with snowy sails outswelled,
Tranquilly glided up the stream, impelled
By the light breeze that blew from off the deep,
As by a shepherdess her milk-white sheep.

And all along the shore was noble shade
By feathery ash and silver poplar made,
Whose hoary trunks the river did reflect,
And giant limbs with wild vines all bedeckt
With ancient vines and tortuous, that upbore
Their knotty, clustered fruit the waters o'er.

Majestically calm, but wearily
And as he fain would sleep, the Rhone passed by
Like some great veteran dying.   He recalls
Music and feasting in Avignon's halls
And castles, and profoundly sad is he
To lose his name and waters in the sea.

Meanwhile the enamoured maiden whom I sing
Had leaped ashore; and the boy, tarrying
Only to say, " The road that lies before
Is thine!   The Saints will guide thee to the door
Of their great chapel," took his oars in hand,
And swiftly turned his shallop from the land.

Under the pouring fire of the June sky,
Like lightning doth Mirèio fly and fly.
East, west, north, south, she seems to see extend
One weary plain, savannas without end,
With glimpses of the sea, and here and there
Tamarisks lifting their light heads in air.

Golden-herb, samphire, shave-grass, soda,—these
Alone grow on the bitter prairies,
Where the black bulls in savage liberty
Rejoice, where the white horses all are free
To roam abroad and breast the briny gale,
Or air surcharged with sea-fog to inhale.

But now o'er all the marsh, dazzling to view,
Soars an immeasurable vault of blue,

Intense, profound. The only living thing
A solitary gull upon the wing
Or hermit-bird whereof the shadow falls
Over the desert meres at intervals,

Or red-legged chevalier, or hern, wild-eyed
With crest of three white plumes upraised in pride.
But soon the sun so beats upon the plain
That the poor, weary wanderer is fain
To loose and lift her folded neckerchief,
So from the burning heat to find relief.

Yet grows the torment ever more and more ;
The sun ascending higher than before,
Till, as a starvèd lion's eye devours
The Abyssinian desert that he scours,
Yon lidless orb the very zenith gains
And pours a flood of fire o'er all the plains.

Now were it sweet beneath a beech to slumber !
Now, like a swarm of hornets without number,—
An angry swarm, fierce darting high and low,—
Or liks the hot sparks from a grindstone, grow
The pitiless rays ; and Love's poor pilgrim, worn
And gasping, and by weariness o'erborne,

Forth from her bodice draws its golden pin,
So that her panting bosom shows within.
All dazzling white, like the campanulas
That bloom beside the summer sea, it was,
And, like twin-billows in a brooklet, full.
Anon, the solitary scene and dull

Loses a little of its sadness, and
A lake shows on the limit of the land,—
A spacious lake, whose wavelets dance and shine,—
While shrnbs of golden-herb and jessamine
On the dark shore appear to soar aloft
Until they cast a shadow cool and soft.

It seems to the poor maid a heavenly vision,
A heartening glimpse into the land elysian.
And soon, afar, by that blue wave she sees
A town with circling walls and palaces,
And fountains gay, and churches without end,
And slender spires that to the sun ascend,

And ships and lesser sailing-craft, sun-bright,
Entering the port ; and the wind seemeth light.
So that the oriflambs and streamers all
Languidly round the masts arise and fall.
" A miracle ! " the maiden thought, and now
Wipes the abundant moisture from her brow,

And, with new hope, toward the town doth fare,
Deeming the Maries' tomb is surely there.
Alas ! alas ! be her flight ne'er so speedy,
A change will pass upon the scene.   Already
The sweet illusion seems to fade and flit ;
Recedes the vision as she follows it.

An airy show, the substance of a dream,
By spirit woven out of a sunbeam,
And all its fair hues borrowed from the sky,—
The filmy fabric wavers presently,
And melts away, and like a mist is gone.
Bewildered by the heat, and quite alone,

Is left Mirèio : yet her way she keeps,
Toiling over the burning, yielding heaps
Of sand ; over the salt-encrusted waste—
Seamed, swollen, dazzling to the eye—doth haste.
On through the tall marsh-grasses and the reeds
And rushes, haunted by the gnat, she speeds,

With Vincen ever in her thought.   And soon,
Skirting the lonesome Vacarès lagune,

She sees it loom at last in distance dim,—
She sees it grow on the horizon's rim,—
The Saints' white tower, across the billowy plain,
Like vessel homeward bound upon the main.

And, even at that blessèd moment, one
Of the hot shafts of the unpitying sun
The ill-starred maiden's forehead pierced, and she
Staggered, death-smitten, by the glassy sea,
And dropped upon the sand. Weep, sons of Crau,
The sweetest flower in all the land lies low.

When, in a valley by the river-side,
Young turtle-doves a huntsman hath espied,
Some innocently drinking, others cooing,
He, through the copse-wood with his gun pursuing,
At the most fair takes alway his first aim,—
The cruel sun had only done the same.

Now, as she lay in swoon upon the shore,
A swarm of busy gnats came hovering o'er,
Who seeing the white breast and fluttering breath,
And the poor maiden fainting to her death,
With ne'er a friendly spray of juniper
From all the pulsing fire to shelter her,

Each one the viol of his tiny wings
Imploring played with plaintive murmurings,—
"Get thee up quickly, quickly, damsel fair !
For aye malignant is this burning air,"
And stung the drooping head ; and sea-spray flew,
Sprinkling the fevered face with bitter dew :

Until at last Mirèio rose again,
And, with a feeble moan of mortal pain,
" My head ! my head ! " she dragged her way forlorn
And slow from salicorne to salicorne,—
Poor little one !—until her heavy feet
Arrived before the seaside Saints' retreat.

There, her sad eyes with tears all brimming o'er,
Upon the cold flags of the chapel-floor,
Wet with the infiltration of the sea,
She sank, and clasped her brow in agony;
And on the pinions of the waiting air
Was borne aloft Mirèio's faltering prayer :—

"O holy Maries, who can cheer
    The sorrow-laden,
Lend, I beseech, a pitying ear
    To one poor maiden !

"And when you see my cruel care
    And misery,
Then look in mercy down the air,
    And side with me !

"I am so young, dear Saints above,
    And there's a youth—
My handsome Vincen—whom I love
    With utter truth !

"I love him as the wayward stream
    Its wanderings;
As loves the new-fledged bird, I deem,
    To try its wings.

"And now they tell me I must quench
    This fire eternal;
Must from the blossoming almond wrench
    Its flowers vernal.

"O holy Maries, who can cheer
    The sorrow-laden,
Lend, I beseech, a pitying ear
    To one poor maiden !

"Now am I come, dear Saints, from far,
    To sue for peace :
Nor mother-prayer my way could bar,
    Nor wilderness;

" The sun, that cruel archer, shot
   Into my brain,—
Thorns, as it were, and nails red-hot,—
   Sharp is the pain ;

" Yet give me but my Vincen dear :
   Then will we duly,
We two, with glad hearts worship here,—
   Oh, I say truly !

" Then the dire pain will rend no more
   These brows of mine,
And the face bathed in tears before
   Will smile and shine.

" My sire mislikes our love ; is cold
   And cruel often :
'Twere naught to you, fair Saints of gold,
   His heart to soften.

" Howe'er so hard the olive grow,
   'Tis mollified
By all the winds that alway blow
   At Advent-tide.

" The medlar and the service-plum,
   So sharp to taste
When gathered, strewn on straw become
   A pleasant feast.

O holy Maries, who can cheer
   The sorrow-laden,
Lend, I beseech, a pitying ear
   To one poor maiden !

 . . . . . .

" Oh, what can mean this dazzling light ?
   The church is riven
O'erhead ; the vault with stars is bright.
   Can this be heaven ?
   G*

"Oh, who so happy now as I?
    The Saints, my God,—
The shining Saints,—toward me fly,
    Down yon bright road !

O blessed patrons, are you there
    To help, to stay me?
Yet hide the dazzling crowns you wear,
    Or these will slay me.

"Veil in a cloud the light appalling !
    My eyes are heavy.
Where is the chapel ?   Are you calling?
    O Saints, receive me ! "

So, in a trance and past all earthly feeling,
The stricken girl upon the pavement kneeling,
With pleading hands, and head thrown backward, cried.
Her large and lovely eyes were opened wide,
As she beyond the veil of flesh discerned
St. Peter's gates, and for the glory yearned.

Mute were her lips now ; but her face yet shone,
And wrapped in glorious contemplation
She seemed. So, when the gold-red rays of dawn
Early alight the poplar-tips upon,
The flickering night-lamp turneth pale and wan
In the dim chamber of a dying man.

And, as at daybreak, also, flocks arouse
From slumber and disperse, the sacred house
Appeared to open, all its vaulted roof
To part, and pillars tall to stand aloof,
Before the three fair women,—heavenly fair,—
Who on a starry path came down the air.

White in the ether pure, and luminous,
Came the three Maries out of heaven thus.

One of them clasped an alabaster vase
Close to her breast, and her celestial face
In splendour had that star alone for peer
That beams on shepherds when the nights are clear.

The next came with a palm in her hand holden,
And the wind lifting her long hair and golden.
The third was young, and wound a mantle white
About her sweet brown visage ; and the light
Of her dark eyes, under their falling lashes,
Was greater than a diamond's when it flashes.

So, nearer to the mourner drew these three,
And leaned above, and spake consolingly.
And bright and tender were the smiles that wreathed
Their lips, and soft the message that they breathed.
They made the thorns of cruel martyrdom,
That pierced Mirèio, into flowers bloom.

✠

"Be of good cheer, thou poor Mirèio ;
For we are they men call the Saints of Baux,—
The Maries of Judæa : and we three—
Be of good cheer !—we watch the stormy sea,
Whereby we succour many a craft distresst ;
For the wild waves are still at our behest.

" Look up along St. James s path in air !
A moment since we stood together there,
At the celestial end thereof, remote,
And, gazing through the clustered stars, took note
How faithful souls to Campoustello throng
To seek the dear Saint's tomb, and worship long.

"And, with the tune of falling fountains blending,
We heard the solemn litanies ascending
From pilgrims gathered in the fields at even,
And pealing of church-bells, and glory given

Unto our son and nephew, by his names
Of Spain's apostle and the greater James.

" Then were we glad of all the pious vows
Paid to his memory ; and, on the brows
Of those poor pilgrims, dews of peace shed we,
And their souls flooded with serenity ;
When, suddenly, thy warm petition came,
And seemed to smite us like a jet of flame.

"Dear child, thy faith is great ; yet thy request
Our pitying hearts right sorely hath opprest.
For thou wouldst drink the waters of pure love,
Or ever to its source thee Death remove,
The bliss we have in God himself to share.
Hast thou, then, seen contentment anywhere

" On earth ?   Is the rich blest, who softly lies,
And in his haughty heart his God denies,
And cares not for his fellow-man at all?
Thou knowest the leech when it is gorged will fall,
And he before the judgment-seat must pass
Of One who meekly rode upon an ass.

" Is the young mother happy to impart
Unto her baby, with a swelling heart,
The first warm jet of milk?   One bitter drop,
Mingled therewith, may poison all her hope.
Now see her lean, distraught, the cradle over,
And a fair little corse with kisses cover.

" And hath she happiness, the promised bride,
Wandering churchward by her lover's side?
Ah, no !   The path under those lingering feet
Thornier shall prove, to those who travel it,
Than sloe-bush of the moorland.   Here below
Are only trial sharp and weary woe.

"And here below the purest waters ever
Are bitter on the lips of the receiver ;
The worm is born within the fruit alway ;
And all things haste to ruin and decay.
The orange thou hast chosen, out of all
The basket's wealth, shall one day taste as gall.

"And in thy world, Mirèio, they who seem
To breathe, sigh only.   And should any dream
Of drinking at the founts that run not dry,
Anguish alone such bitter draught will buy.
So must the stone be broken evermore,
Ere thou extract the shining silver ore.

"Happy is he who cares for others' woe,
And toils for men, and wearies only so ;
From his own shoulders tears their mantle warm,
Therein to fold some pale and shivering form ;
Is lowly with the lowly, and can waken
Fire-light on cold hearths of the world-forsaken.

"Hark to the sovereign word, of man forgot,
'Death too is Life ; ' and happy is the lot
Of the meek soul and simple,—he who fares
Quietly heavenward, wafted by soft airs ;
And lily-white forsakes this low abode,
Where men have stoned the very saints of God.

"And if, Mirèio, thou couldst see before thee,
As we from empyrean heights of glory,
This world ; and what a sad and foolish thing
Is all its passion for the perishing,
Its churchyard terrors,—then, O lambkin sweet,
Mayhap thou wouldst for death and pardon bleat !

"But, ere the wheat-ear hath its feathery birth,
Ferments the grain within the darksome earth,—

Such ever is the law ; and even we,
Before we wore our crowns of majesty,
Drank bitter draughts.   Therefore, thy soul to stay,
We'll tell the pains and perils of our way."

Paused for a moment, then, the holy three.
The waves, being fain to listen, coaxingly
Had flocked along the ocean sand ; the pines
Unto the rustling water-weeds made signs ;
And teal and gull beheld, with deep amaze,
Peace on the restless heart of Vacarès ;

The sun and moon, afar the desert o'er,
Bow their great crimson foreheads, and adore ;
And all Camargue—salt-sown, forsaken isle—
Seems thrilled with sacred expectation ; while
The saints, to hearten for her mortal strife
Love's martyr, tell the story of their life.

The Saints.

" THE cross was looming yet, Mirèio,
    Aloft on the Judæan mount of woe,
Wet with the blood of God ;.and all the time
Seemed crying to the city of the crime,
' What hast thou done, thou lost and slumbering—
What hast thou done, I say, with Bethlehem's King ? '

" The angry clamours of the streets were stayed :
Cedron alone a low lamenting made
Afar ; and Jordan rolled a gloomy tide,
Hasting into the desert, there to hide
The overflowings of his grief and rage
'Mid terebinth and lentisk foliage.

" And all the poorer folk were heavy-hearted,
Knowing it was the Christ who had departed,
First having opened his own prison-door,
On friends and followers to look once more,
The sacred keys unto St. Peter given,
And, like an eagle, soared away to heaven.

" Oh ! then in Jewry woe and weeping were
For the fair Galilean carpenter,—
Him who His honeyed parables distilled
Over their hearts, and fainting thousands filled
Upon the hillsides with unleavened bread,
And healed the leper and revived the dead.

" But scribes and kings and priests, and all the horde
Of sacrilegious vendors whom the Lord
Had driven from his house, their hatred uttered,
' And who the people will restrain,' they muttered,
' Unless in all the region round about
The glory of this cross be soon put out ? '

" So raged they, and the martyrs testified :
Stephen the first was stoned until he died,
James with the sword was slain, and many a one
Cruelly crushed beneath a weight of stone.
Yet, dying, all bear record undismayed :
' Christ Jesus is the Son of God ! ' they said.

" Then us, brothers and sisters of the slain,
Who him had followed in a loving train,
They thrust into a crazy bark ; and we,
Oarless and sailless, drifted out to sea.
We women sorely wept, the men their eyes
Anxiously lifted to the lowering skies.

" Palaces, temples, olive-trees, we saw—
Swiftly, oh swiftly !—from our gaze withdraw,
All saving Carmel's rugged crests, and those
But as a wave on the horizon rose.
When suddenly a sharp cry toward us drifted.
We turned, and saw a maid with arms uplifted.

" ' Oh, take me with you ! ' cried she in distress ;
' Oh, take me in the bark, my mistresses,
With you !   I, too, must die for Jesus' sake ! '
It was our handmaid Sarah thus who spake.
Up there in heaven, whither she is gone,
She shineth sweetly as an April dawn !

" Seaward before the wind our vessel drave.
Then God a thought unto Salome gave :

Her veil upon the foamy deep she threw,—
Oh, wondrous faith!—and on the water, blue
And white commingling wildly, it sustained
The maid until our fragile craft she gained,

" To her as well the strong breeze lending aid.
Now saw we in the hazy distance fade,
Hill-top by hill-top, our dear native land ;
The sea encompassed us on every hand ;
And a sharp home-sickness upon us fell,
The pangs whereof he who hath felt may tell.

" So must we say farewell, O sacred shore !
O doomed Judæa, farewell evermore !
Thy just are banished, thy God crucified !
Henceforth let serpents in thy halls abide ;
And wandering lions, tawny, terrible,
Feed on thy vines and dates.   Farewell ! farewell !

" The gale had grown into a tempest now :
The vessel fled before it.   On the prow
Martial was kneeling, and Saturnius :
While, in his mantle folded, Trophimus
The aged saint silently meditated ;
And Maximin the bishop near him waited.

" High on the main-deck Lazarus held his place.
There was an awful pallor on his face,—
Hues of the winding-sheet and of the grave.
He seemed to face the anger of the wave.
Martha his sister to his side had crept,
And Magdalene behind them cowered and wept.

" The slender bark, pursued of demons thus,
Contained, beside, Cléon, Eutropius,
Marcellus, Joseph of Arimathea,
Sidonius.   And sweet it was to hear
The psalms they sang on the blue waste of sea,
Leaned o'er the tholes.   Te Deum, too, said we.

" How rushed the boat the sparkling billows by !
E'en yet that sea seems present to the eye.
The breeze, careering, on the waters hurled,
Whereby the snowy spray was tossed and whirled,
And lifted in light wreaths into the air,
That soared like souls aloft, and vanished there.

" Out of the waves at morning rose the Sun,
And set therein when his day's course was run.
Mere waifs were we upon the briny plain,
The sport of all the winds that scour the main ;
Yet of our God withheld from all mischance,
That we might bear His gospel to Provence.

" At last there came a morning still and bright.
We noted how, with lamp in hand, the night
Most like an anxious widow from us fled,
Risen betimes to turn her household bread
Within the oven.   Ocean seemed as napping,
The languid waves the boatside barely tapping.

' Till a dull, bellowing noise assailed the ear.
Unknown before, it chilled our blood to hear.
And next we marked a strange, upheaving motion
Upon the utmost limit of the ocean,
And, stricken speechless by the gathering roar,
Helplessly gazed the troubled waters o'er.

" Then saw we all the deep with horror lower,
As the swift squall descended in its power ;
The waves drop dead still,—'twas a portent fell ;
The bark hang motionless, as by a spell
Entranced ; and far away, against the skies,
A mountain of black water seemed to rise,

" And all the heaped-up sea, with vapour crested,
To burst upon our vessel, thus arrested.

God, 'twas an awful hour !   One monster wave
Seemed thrusting us into a watery grave,
Fainting to death.   Or ever it closed o'er us,
The next upon a dizzy height upbore us.

"The lightning cleft the gloom with blades of fire ;
Peal followed peal of thunder, deafening, dire.
It was as if all hell had been unchained
Upon our tiny craft, which groaned and strained
So hunted, and seemed rushing on her wreck,
And smote our foreheads with her heaving deck.

" Now rode we on the shoulders of the main ;
Now sank into its inky gulfs again,
Where the seal dwelleth and the mighty shark,
And the sea-peacock ; and we seemed to hark
To the sad cry, lifted unceasingly,
By the unresting victims of the sea.

" A great wave brake above us, and hope died.
Then Lazarus prayed : 'O Lord, be thou our guide,
Who me ere now out of the tomb didst bring !
Succour the bark, for she is foundering !'
Like a wood-pigeon's wing, this outcry clove
The tempest, and went up to realms above.

"And Jesus, looking from the palace fair
Where he sat throned, beheld his friend's despair,
And the fierce deep yawning to swallow him.
Straightway the Master's gentle eyes grew dim,
His heart yearned over us with pity warm,
And one long sun-ray leaped athwart the storm.

" Now God be praised !   For, though we yet were tost
Right roughly up and down, and sank almost
With bitter sea-sickness, our fears were stayed :
The haughty waves began to be allayed ;
Clouds brake afar, then vanished altogether,
And a green shore gleamed through the bright'ning
    weather.

" Long was it yet ere the shocks quite subsided
Of the tempestuous waves ; and our boat glided
Our crazy boat, nearer that welcome shore
All tranquilly, a dying breeze before.
Smooth as a grebe our keel the breakers clomb,
Furrowing into great flakes the snowy foam.

" Until—once more all glory be to God !—
Upon a rockless beach we safely trod,
And knelt on the wet sand, and cried, ' O Thou
Who saved from sword and tempest, hear our vow !
Each one of us is an evangelist
Thy law to preach.   We swear it, O Lord Christ !'

" At that great name, that cry till then unheard,
Noble Provence, wert thou not deeply stirred ?
Thy woods and fields, in all their fair extent,
Thrilled with the rapture of a sweet content ;
As a dog scents his master's coming feet,
And flies with bounding welcome him to meet.

" Thou, Heavenly Father, also didst provide
A feast of shell-fish, stranded by the tide,
To stay our hunger ; and, to quench our thirst,
Madest among the salicornes outburst
The same clear, healing spring, which flows alway
Inside the church where sleeps our dust to-day.

" Glowing with zeal, we track the shingly Rhone
From moor to moor.   In faith we travel on
Until right gladly we discern the traces
Of human husbandry in those wild places,
And soon, afar, the tall Arlesian towers,
Crowned by the standard of the emperors.

" To-day, fair Arles, a harvester thou seemest,
Who sleepest on thy threshing-floor, and dreamest

Of glories past ; but a queen wert thou then,
And mother of so brave sea-faring men,
The noisy winds themselves aye lost their way
In the great harbour where thy shipping lay.

" Rome had arrayed thee in white marble newly,
As an imperial princess decked thee duly.
Thy brow a crown of stately columns wore ;
The gates of thy arena were sixscore ;
Thou hadst thy theatre and hippodrome,
So to make mirth in thy resplendent home !

" We pass within the gates.   A crowd advances
Toward the theatre, with songs and dances.
We join them ; and the eager thousands press
Through the cool colonnades of palaces ;
As.thou, mayhap, a mighty flood hast seen
Rush through a maple-shaded, deep ravine.

" Arrived,—oh, shame and sorrow !—we saw there
On the proscenium, with bosoms bare,
Young maidens waltzing to a languid lyre,
And high refrain sung by a shrill-voiced choir.
They in the mazes of their dance surrounded
A marble shape, whose name like ' Venus ' sounded.

" The frenzied populace its clamour adds
Unto the cries of lasses and of lads,
Who shout their idol's praises o'er and o'er,—
' Hail to the Venus, of joy the bestower !
Hail to thee, Venus, goddess of all grace !
Mother of earth and of the Arlesian race ! '

" The statue, myrtle-crowned, with nostrils wide
And head high-borne, appears to swell with pride
Amid the incense-clouds ; when suddeniy,
In horror of so great audacity,
Leaps Trophimus amid the maddened wretches,
And o'er the bewildered throng his arms outstretches.

" ' People of Arles ! ' in mighty tones he cried,
' Hear me, even for the sake of Christ who died
No more.   But, smitten by his shaggy frown,
The idol groaned and staggered, and fell down,
Headlong, from off its marble pedestal.
Fell, too, the awe-struck dancers, one and all.

" Therewith went up, as 'twere, a single howl
Choked were the gateways with a rabble foul,
Who filled all Arles with terror and dismay,
So that patricians tore their crowns away ;
And all the enragèd youth closed round us there,
While flashed a thousand poniards in the air.

" Yet they recoiled ;—whether it were the sight
Of us, in our salt-crusted robes bedight ;
Or Trophimus' calm brow which beamed on them,
As wreathed with a celestial diadem ;
Or tear-veiled Magdalene, who stood between us,—
How tenfold fairer than their sculptured Venus !

" And the old saint resumed : ' Arlesian men,
Hear ye my message first ; and slay me then,
If need be.   Ye have seen your goddess famed
Shiver like glass when my God was but named :
Deem not, Arlesians, that the thing was wrought
By my poor, feeble voice ; for we are naught.

" ' The God who thus your idol smote, but now
No lofty temple hath on the hill's brow ;
But Day and Night see him alone up there !
And stern to sin, but generous to prayer,
Is he ; and he hath made, with his own hand,
The sky, the sea, the mountains, and the land.

" ' One day he saw, from his high dwelling-place,
All his good things devoured by vermin base ;

Slaves who drank hatred with their tears, and had
No comforter; and Evil, priestly clad,
At altars keeping school; and, in the street,
Maids who ran out the libertines to meet.

" ' Wherefore, to purge this vileness, and to end
Man's torment and our pilloried race befriend,
He sent his own Son out of heaven down.
Naked and poor, wearing no golden crown,
He came, was of a virgin born, and saw
The daylight first pillowed on stable-straw.

" ' People of Arles, turn to this lowly One.
Ourselves can show the wonders he hath done,
Who were his comrades; and, in that far land
Where rolls the yellow Jordan, saw him stand,
In his white linen robe, amid the crowd,
Who him assailed with maledictions loud.

" ' Full gentle was his message : for he showed
That men should love each other, and that God
Is both almighty and all merciful ;
And that the kingdom where he beareth rule
Descendeth not to tyrants, cheats, and scorners,
But to the poor, the lowly, and the mourners.

" ' These were his teachings : and he them attested
By walking on the waters ; and arrested
Sickness most bitter by a glance, a word.
The dead, by yon grim rampart undeterred,
Came back to earth.   This Lazarus whom you see
Once rotted in the grave.   But jealousy

" ' Inflamed the bad hearts of the Jewish kings.
They led him to a mountain for these things,
And cruelly unto a tree trunk nailed,
Spat on the sacred face, and coarsely railed
And lifted him on high.'   Here all the throng
Brake into loud lament and sobbing strong.

" ' Mercy,' they cried, ' for our iniquities !
What shall we do the Father to appease ?
Answer us, man of God !   If blood must flow,
He shall have hecatombs."—' Ah, no ! ah, no ! '
Replied the saint ; ' but slay before the Father
Your vices and your evil passions rather ! '

" So knelt, and prayed : ' Lord, thou dost not desire
Odour of slaying, sacrificial fire,
Or stately temples !   Dearer far to thee
Is the bread given to those who fainting be ;
Or sweet girl's timid coming, who doth bring
Her pure heart, like a May-flower, to her king.'

" As o'er the Apostle's lips, like sacred oil,
The word of God was flowing, 'gan recoil
The idols everywhere, and plunged at last
Adown the temple stairs ; while tears dropped fast,
And rich and poor and working-men all ran
To kiss the garment of the holy man.

" Then bare Sidonius witness.   In his night—
He was born blind—he led to the true light
The men of Arles.   And Maximin, beside,
The resurrection of the Crucified
Set forth, and bade them turn from sin away.
Arles was baptized upon that very day.

" Then the Lord's breath did speed us in our going,
Like wind upon a fire of shavings blowing ;
For, as we turned of these to take farewell,
Came messengers, before our feet who fell,
And passionately cried, ' O god-sent strangers !
Hear yet the story of our cruel dangers.

' ' To our unhappy city came the sound
Of marvels wrought and oracles new found.

She sends us hither. We are dead who stand
Before you ! Such a monster wastes our land !
A scourge of God, greedy of human gore,
It haunts our woods and gorges. We implore

" ' Your help. The monster hath a dragon's tail,
Bristles its back with many a horrid scale.
It hath six human feet, and fleet they are ;
A lion's jaw ; eyes red like cinnabar.
Its prey it hideth in a cavern lone,
Under a rock that beetles o'er the Rhone.

" ' Now day by day our fishermen grow few
And fewer.' Saying this, they wept anew
And bitterly,—the men of Tarascon.
Then maiden Martha said, serene and strong,
' Ready am I, and my heart yearns with pity.
Marcellus, haste : we two will save the city ! '

" For the last time on earth we did embrace,
With hope of meeting in a happy place,
And parted. Martial to Limoges him hied,
While fair Toulouse became Saturnius' bride :
And our Eutropius the new cause did plead,
And sow, in brave Orange, the blessèd seed.

" And thou, sweet virgin, whither goest thou ?
With step unfaltering and untroubled brow,
Martha her cross and holy-water carried
Against the dragon dire, and never tarried.
The wild men clomb the pine-trees round about,
The fray to witness and the maiden's rout.

" Startled from slumber in his darksome cave,
Thou shouldst have seen the leap the monster gave
Yet vainly writhed he 'neath the holy dew,
And growled and hissed as Martha near him drew,
Bound with a frail moss-halter, and forth led
Snorting. Then all the people worshippèd.

H

" ' Huntress Diana art thou ? ' prostrate falling
Before the Christian maid, began they calling ;
' Or yet Minerva, the all-wise and chaste ? '
' Nay, nay ! ' the damsel answered in all haste :
' I am God's handmaid only.' And the crowd
She taught until with her to Him they bowed.

" Then by the power of her young voice alone,
She smote Avignon's rock ; and from the stone
Welled faith in so pellucid stream, that, later,
Clements and Gregories in that fair water
Dipped holy chalices their thirst to slake,
And Rome long years did for her glory quake.

" And all Provence, regenerate, sang so clear
A hymn of praise, that God was glad to hear.
Hast thou not marked, when rain begins to fall,
How spring the drooping trees and grasses all,
How soon the foliage with joy will quiver ?
So fevered souls drank of this cooling river !

" Thou fair Marseilles, who openest on the sea
Thy haughty eyes and gazest languidly,
As though naught else were worthy to behold,
And, though the winds rage, dreamest but of gold,
When Lazarus preached to thee, thou didst begin
Those eyes to close, and see the night within,

" And to the sources of that river speeding,
That aye the tears of Magdalene were feeding,
Didst wash thy sins away : and in this hour
Art proud once more ; but other storms may lower.
Forget not, then, amid thy revelries,
Whose tears they are that bathe thine olive-trees !

" Dark cedars that on Mount Sambuco grew,
Sheer ledges of the hills of Aix, and you,

Tall pines, clothing the flanks of Esterel,
And junipers of Trevaresso, tell
How thrilled your vales with joy, when, his cross bearing,
The bishop Maximin was through them faring.

" Seest thou one with white arms on her breast,
Who kneels and prays in yonder grotto, dressed
In the bright garment of her floating hair ?
Poor sufferer ! Her tender knees are bare,
And cruelly by the sharp flints are torn.
The moon, with pale torch, watches the forlorn

" And sad recluse. The woods in silence bow.
The angels hush their very heart-throbs now,
As, gazing through a crevice, they espy
A pearly tear fall from the lifted eye,
And haste the precious gem to gather up,
And keep for ever in a golden cup.

" Enough, O Magdalene ! Thirty years ago,
The wind that in the forest whispers low
Bare thee the pardon of the Man divine !
The tears that the rock weeps are tears of thine.
These, like a snowfall softly sprinkled o'er,
Shall whiten woman's love for ever more !

" But naught can stay the mourner's gnawing grief.
Even the little birds bring not relief,
That flock around her, building many a nest
On Saint Pilon ; nor spirits of the blest,
Who lift and rock her in their arms of love,
And soar, seven times a day, the vales above.

" O Lord, be thine the glory ! And may we
In thy full brightness and reality
Behold thee ever ! Poor and fugitive,
We women did of thy great grace receive.

We, even we, touched by thy love supernal,
Shed some faint reflex of the light eternal.

"Ye, Alpine peaks and all blue hills of Baux,
Unto the latest hour of time will show
The traces of our teaching carved in stone !
And so Death found us on the marshes lone,
Deep in Camargue, encircled by the sea,
And from our day's long labour set us free.

"And as, on earth, haste all things to decay,
Faded the memory of our tombs away.
While sang Provence her songs, and time rolled on,
Till, as Durance is blended with the Rhone,
Ended the merry kingdom of Provence,
And fell asleep upon the breast of France.

" ' France, take thy sister by the hand ! '   So saith
Our land's last king, he drawing near to death.
' On the great work the future hath in store,
Together counsel take !   Thou art the more
Strong ; she, the more fair : and rebel night
Before your wedded glory shall take flight.'

"This did Renè.   Therefore we sought the king,
As on his feathers he lay slumbering,
And showed the spot where long our bones had lain ;
And he, with bishops twelve and courtly train,
Came down into this waste of sand and waves,
And found, among the salicornes, our graves.

"Adieu, dear Mirèio !   The hour flies ;
And, like a taper's flame before it dies,
We see life's light within thy body flicker.
Yet, ere the soul is loosed,—come quick, oh quicker,
My sisters !—we the hills of heaven must scale
Or ever she arrive within the veil.

" Roses and a white robe we must prepare !
She is love's martyr and a virgin fair
Who dies to-day !   With sweetest flowers blow,
Celestial paths ! and on Mirèio
Shine saintly splendours of the heavenly host !
Glory to Father, Son, and Holy Ghost ! "

CANTO XII.

Death.

A S, when in orange-lands God's day is ending,
   The maids let fly the leafy boughs, and, lending
A helpful hand, the laden baskets lift
On head or hip, and fishing-boats adrift
Are drawn ashore, and, following the sun,
The golden clouds evanish, one by one ;

As the full harmonies of eventide,
Swelling from hill and plain and river-side
Along the sinuous Argens,—airy notes
Of pastoral pipe, love-songs, and bleat of goats,—
Grow fainter, and then wholly fade away,
And sombre night falls on the mountains gray ;

Or as the last sigh of an anthem soft,
Or dying organ-peal, is borne aloft
O'er some old church, and on the wandering wind
Passes afar,—so passed the music twined
Of the three Maries' voices, heavenward carried.
For her, she seemed asleep ; for yet she tarried

Kneeling : and was more fair than ever now,
So strange a freak of sunlight crowned her brow.
And here they who had sought her through the wild,
The aged parents, came, and found their child ;
Yet stayed their faltering steps the portal under,
To gaze on her entranced with awe and wonder ;

Then crossed their foreheads with the holy water,
And, hasting o'er the sounding flags, besought her
To wake. But, as a frighted vireo
Who spies the huntsman, shrieked Mirèio,
" O God, what is it ? Father, mother, tell !
Where will you go ?" And therewith swooned and fell.

The weeping mother lifts her head, and yearns
Over her. " My sweet, your forehead burns !
What means it ?" And again, " No dream is this.
My own sweet child,—my very own it is,—
Low lying at my feet !" And then she wept
And laughed together ; and old Ramoun crept

Beside them. " Little darling, it is I,
Your father, has your hand !" Then suddenly
His anguish choked him, and he could but hold
And chafe and strive to warm those fingers cold.
Meanwhile the wind the mournful tidings bore
Abroad, and all Li Santo thronged the door,

And anxiously. " Bear the sick child," they say,
" Into the upper chapel, nor delay ;
And let her touch the dear Saints' relics thus
Within their reliquaries marvellous ;
Or kiss, at least, with dying lips !" And there
Two women raised, and bore her up the stair.

In this fair church, altars and chapels three,
Built one upon the other, you may see,
Of solid stone. In that beneath the ground
The dusky gypsies kneel, with awe profound,
Before Saint Sarah. One is over it
That hath God's altar. And one higher yet,

On pillars borne,—last of the sanctuaries,—
The small, funereal chapel of the Maries,

With heavenward vault.   And here long years have lain
Rich legacy,—whence falleth grace like rain !—
The ever-blessed relics.   Four great keys
Enlock the cypress chests that shelter these.

Once are they opened in each hundred years ;
And happy, happy shall he be who nears
And sees and touches them !   Upon the wave
Bright star and weather fair his bark shall have,
His trees be with abundant fruitage graced,
His faithful soul eternal blessing taste !

An oaken door, with carvings rich and rare,
Gift of the pious people of Beaucaire,
Closes the holy precinct.   And yet surely
That which defends is not the portal purely,—
Is not the circling rampart ; but the grace
Descending from the azure depths of space.

So to the chapel bare they the sick child,
While up the winding stair the folk defiled ;
And, as a white-robed priest threw wide the door,
They, entering, fell on the dusty floor,
As falls full-bearded barley when a squall
Hath smitten it, and worshipped one and all.

" O lovely Saints ! O friendly Saints ! " they said,
" O Saints of God, pity this poor young maid ! "
" Pity her ! " sobbed the mother.   " I will bring,
When she is well, so fair an offering !
My flower-carved cross, my golden ring ! " she cried,
" And tell the tale through town and country-side ! "

" O Saints," groaned Ramoun, stumbling in the gloom
While shook his aged head, " be kind, and come !
Look on this little one !   She is my treasure !
She is my plover !   Pretty beyond measure,
And good and meet for life !   Send my old bones
To dung the mallows, but save her ! " he moans.

And all the while Mirèio lay in swoon,
Till a breeze, with declining afternoon,
Blew from the tamarisks. Then, hoping still
To call her back to life, they raised with skill,
The flower of Lotus Farm, and tenderly
Laid on the tiles that overlook the sea.

There, from the doorway leading on the tiles,—
The chapel's eye,—one's vision roams for miles,
Even to the pallid limit of the brine,
The blending and the separating line
Between the clouds and waters to explore,
And the great waves that roll for evermore.

Insensate and unceasing and untiring,
They follow one another on ; expiring,
With sullen roar, amid the drifted sand :
While vast savannas, on the other hand,
Stretch till they meet a heaven without a stain,
Unfathomed blue over unmeasured plain.

Only a light-green tamarisk, here and there,
Quivering in the faintest breath of air,
Or a long belt of salicornes, appears,
With swans that dip them in the desert meres,
With oxen roaming the waste moor at large;
Or swimming Vacares from marge to marge.

At last the maiden murmured, but how weak
The voice ! how vague the words !   " On either cheek
I seem to feel a breeze,—one from the sea,
One from the land : and this refreshes me
Like morning airs ; but that doth sore oppress
And burn me, and is full of bitterness."

So ceased.   The people of Li Santo turn
Blankly from plain to ocean : then discern

A lad who nears them, at so fleet a pace
The dust in clouds is raised; and, in the race
Outstripped, the tamarisks are growing small,
And far behind the runner seem to fall.

Vincen it was.   Ah, poor unhappy youth!
When Master Ambroi spake that sorry truth,
" My son, the pretty little lotus-spray
Is not for you!" he turned, and fled away;
From Valabrègo like a bandit fled,
To see her once again.   And when they said

In Crau, " She in Li Santo must be sought,"
Rhone, marshes, weary Crau, withheld him not;
Nor stayed he ever in his frantic search
Till, seeing that great throng inside the church,
He rose on tiptoe deadly pale, and crying,
" Where is she?"   And they answered, " She is dying

" Above there in the chapel."   In despair
And all distraught, he hurried up the stair;
But, when his eye fell on the prostrate one,
Threw his hands wildly up.   " What have I done,—
What have I done against my God and hers
To call down on me such a heavy curse

" From Heaven?   Have I cut the throat of her
Who gave me birth? or at a church taper
Lighted my pipe? or dared I, like the Jews,
The holy crucifix 'mong thistles bruise?
What is it, thou accursèd year of God,—
Why must I bear so terrible a load?

" 'Twas not enough my darling they denied
To me!   They've hunted her to death!" he cried;
And then he knelt, and kissed her passionately;
And all the people, when they saw how greatly
His heart was wrung, felt theirs too swell with pain,
And wept aloud above the stricken twain.

Then, as the sound of many waters, falling
Far down a rocky valley, rises calling
Unto the shepherd high the hills among,
Rose from the church a sound of full-choired song,
And all the temple trembled with the swell
Of that sweet psalm the Santen sing so well :—

    " Saints of God, ere now sea-faring
      On these briny plains of ours,
    Who have set a temple bearing
      Massy walls and snowy towers,

    " Watch the wave-tossed seaman kindly ;
      Lend him aid the bark to guide ;
    Send him fair winds, lest he blindly
      Perish on the pathless tide !

    " See the woman poor and sightless :
      Ne'er a word she uttereth ;
    Dark her days are and delightless,—
      Darkness aye is worse than death.

    " Vain the spells they have told o'er her,
      Blank is all her memory.
    Queens of Paradise, restore her !
      Touch those eyes that they may see !

    " We who are but fishers lowly,
      Lift our hearts ere forth we go ;
    Ye, the helpful saints and holy,
      Fill our nets to overflow.

    " So, when penitents heart-broken,
      Sue for pardon at your door,
    Flood their souls with peace unspoken,
      White flowers of our briny moor ! "

So prayed the Santen, with tears and strong crying.
Then came the patrons to the maid low-lying,
And breathed a little life into her frame ;
So that her wan eyes brightened, and there came
A tender flush of joy her visage over,
At the sweet sight of Vincen bent over her.

" Why love, whence came you ?   Do you mind, I pray,
A word you said down at the Farm one day,
Walking under the trellis, by my side?
You said, ' If ever any harm betide,
Hie thee right quickly to the holy Saints,
Who cure all ills and hearken all complaints."

" Dearest, I would you saw my heart this minute,
As in a glass, and all the comfort in it !
Comfort and peace like a full fountain welling
Through all my happy spirit !   There's no telling—
A grace beyond my uttermost desires !
Look, Vincen : see you not God's angel-choirs ? "

Pausing, she gazed into the deep blue air.
It was as if she could discern up there
Wonderful things hidden from mortal men.
But soon her dreamy speech began again :
" Ah, they are happy, happy souls that soar
Aloft, tethered by flesh to earth no more !

" Did you mark, Vincen dear, the flakes of light
That fell when they began their heavenward flight ?
If all their words to me had written been,
They would have made a precious book, I ween."
Here Vincen, who had striven his tears to stay,
Brake forth in sobs, and gave his anguish way.

" Would to God I *had* seen them ere they went !
Ah, would to God !   Then to their white raiment,

Like a tick fastening, I would have cried,
' O queens of heaven ! Sole ark where we may bide,
In this late hour, do what you will with me !
Maimed, sightless, toothless, I would gladly be ;

" ' But leave my pretty little fairy sane
And sound ! ' " Here brake Mirèio in again :
" There are they, in their linen robes of grace !
They come ! " and from her mother's fond embrace
Began to struggle wildly to be free,
And waved her hand afar toward the sea.

Then all the folk turned also to the main,
And under shading hands their eyes 'gan strain ;
Yet, save the pallid limit of the brine,.
The blending and the separating line
'Twixt wave and vault, they nothing could descry.
" Naught cometh," said they. But the child, " Oh, ay !

" Look closer ! There's a bark, without a sail,
Wafted toward us by a gentle gale,
And they are on it ! And the swell subsides
Before them, and the bark so softly glides !
Clear is the air and all the sea like glass,
And the sea-birds do homage as they pass ! "

" Poor child ! she wanders," murmured they ; " for we
See only the red sunset on the sea ! "
" Yet it is they ! Mine eyes have told me true,"
The sick one panted—" 'Tis the boat in view !
Now low, now lifted, it is drawing near,
Oh, miracle of God !—the boat is here ! "

Now was she paling, as a marguerite
Half-blown and smitten by a tropic heat,
While crouching Vincen, horror in his heart,
Or ere his well-belovèd quite depart
Hath her in charge unto our Lady given,
To the Saints of the chapel and of heaven.

Lit are the tapers, and, in violet stole
Begirt, the priest, to stay the passing soul,
Lays angel's bread to those dry lips of hers,
And the last unction so administers ;
Then of her body the seven parts anoints
With holy oil, as holy church appoints.

The hour was calm.   Upon the tiles no word
Save the *oremus* of the priest was heard.
The last red shaft of the declining day
Struck on the wall and passed, and heaven turned gray.
The sea's long waves came slowly up the shore,
Brake with a murmur soft, and were no more.

Beside the maid knelt father, mother, lover,
And hoarsely sobbed at intervals above her ;
Till once again her lips moved, and she spake :
"Now is the parting close at hand !   So take
My hand, and press it quickly, dears.   Lo, now
The glory grows on either Mary's brow !

" The pink flamingoes flock from the Rhone shore,
The tamarisks in blossom all adore.
The dear Saints beckon me to them," she said.
" They tell me I need never be afraid :
They know the constellations of the skies ;
Their bark will take us quick to Paradise !"

" My little pet," said Ramoun, quite undone,
"You will not go, and leave the home so lone !
Why have I felled my oaks with such ado?
The zeal that nerved me only came of you.
If the hot sun on sultry glebe o'ertook me,
I thought of you, and heat and thirst forsook me."

" Dear father, if a moth shall sometime fly
About your lamp at night, that will be I.

But see ! the Saints are standing on the prow !
They wait.   I'm coming in a moment now !
Slowly I move, good Saints, for I am ailing."
" It is too much ! " the mother brake out, wailing.

" Oh, stay with me !   I cannot let you die.
And, when you're well, Mirèio, by and by
We'll go some day to Aunt Aurano's, dear,
And carry pomegranates.   Do you hear ?
Maiano is not distant from our home ;
And, in one day, one may both go and come."

" Not very distant, mother,—that I know ;
But all alone thou wilt the journey go !
Now give me my white raiment, mother mine.
Oh, how the mantles of the Maries shine !
Sawest thou ever such a dazzling sight ?
The snow upon the hillsides is less white ! "

" O thou," cried the dark weaver, " who didst ope
The palace of thy love to me, my hope,
My queen, my all !   A blossoming alms thou gavest ;
The mire of my low life in thine thou lavest,
Till it shines like a mirror, and dost place
Me in eternal honour by thy grace.

" Pearl of Provence ! of my young days the sun !
Shall it be ever said of such an one,
I saw upon her forehead the death-dew ?
Shall it be said, puissant Saints, of you,
You looked unmoved upon her mortal pain,
Letting her clasp your sacred sill in vain ? "

Slowly the maiden answered, " My poor friend,
What is it doth affright you, and offend ?
Believe me, dear, the thing that we call death
Is a delusion.   Lo ! it vanisheth,
As a fog when the bells begin their pealing ;
As dreams with daylight through the window stealing.

" I am not dying ! See, I mount the boat
With a light foot l And now we are afloat !
Good-by ! good-by ! We are drifting out to sea.
The waves encompass us, and needs must be
The very avenue to Paradise,
For all around they touch the azure skies !

"Gently they rock us now.   And overhead
So many stars are shining ! Ah," she said,
" Among those worlds one surely may be found
Where two may love in peace !   Hark, Saints, that
    sound !
Is it an organ played across the deep?"
Then sighed, and fell, as it had been, asleep.

And, by her smiling lips, you might have guessed
That yet she spake.   Only the Santen pressed
About the sleeper in a mournful band,
And, with a taper passed from hand to hand,
Signed the cross o'er her.   While, as turned to stone,
The parents gazed on what themselves had done.

To them her form is all enrayed with light.
Vainly they feel her cold, they see her white :
The awful stroke they comprehend not now.
But, soon as Vincen marked the level brow,
The rigid arms, the sweet eyes wholly veiled,
" See you not she is dead?" he loudly wailed.

" Quite dead?" And therewith fiercely wrung his
    hands,
As he of old had wrung the osier-strands,
And threw his naked arms abroad.   " My own ! "
He cried, " they will not weep for you alone :
With yours, the trunk of my life too they fell.
' Dead ' was I saying?   'Tis impossible :

" A demon whispered me the word, no doubt !
Tell me, in God's name, ye who stand about,—
Ye who have seen dead women ere to-day,—
If, passing through the gates, they smile that way.
Her look is well-nigh merry, do you see ?
Why do they turn their heads away from me,

" And weep ? This means, I think, that all is o'er.
Her pretty prattle I shall hear no more :
Still is the voice I loved ! " All hearts were thrilled ;
Tears rushed like rain, and sobs would not be stilled.
One sound went up of weeping and lament,
Till the waves on the beach returned the plaint.

So when in some great herd a heifer dies,
About the carcass where it starkly lies
Nine following eves the beasts take up their station,
And seem to mourn after their speechless fashion ;
The sea, the plain, the winds, thereover blowing,
Echo nine days with melancholy lowing,—

" Poor Master Ambroi ! " Vincen wandered on,
" Thou wilt weep heavy tears over thy son !
And now, good Santen, one last wish is mine,—
Bury me with my love, below the brine ;
Scoop in the oozy sand a crib for two :
Tears for so great a mourning will not do.

" And a stone wall about the basin set,
So the sea flow not in, and part us yet !
Santen, I trust you ! Then, while they are beating
Their brows, and with remorse her name repeating,
There at the farm where her home used to be,
Far from the unrest of the upper sea,

" Down in the peaceful blue we will abide,
My oh so pretty, alway side by side ;

I

And you shall tell me of your Maries over,
Over, until with shells the great storms cover."
Here the crazed weaver on the corse him threw,
And from the church arose the psalm anew.

.   .   .   .   .   .

" So, when penitents heart-broken
    Sue for pardon at your door,
  Flood their souls with peace unspoken,
    White flowers of our briny moor ! "

www.ingramcontent.com/pod-product-compliance
Lightning Source LLC
Chambersburg PA
CBHW030845270326
41928CB00007B/1227